A
Wiltshire
Christmas

Compiled by John Chandler

ALAN SUTTON PUBLISHING LIMITED

First published in the United Kingdom in 1991 by
Alan Sutton Publishing Limited · Phoenix Mill · Far Thrupp
Stroud · Gloucestershire

Reprinted 1995

British Library Cataloguing in Publication Data

Chandler, John H. (John Howard), *1951–*
A Wiltshire Christmas.
I. Title
394.26828209431

ISBN 0-86299-929-4

Cover illustration: A Wintry Walk *by Charles Leaver (photograph
courtesy Fine Art Photographs)*

Typeset in Garamond 12/13.
Typesetting and origination by
Alan Sutton Publishing Limited.
Printed in Great Britain by
WBC Ltd, Bridgend.

Christmas comes to a Wiltshire Village

HEATHER TANNER

'Kington Borel is not to be found on the map', wrote Heather Tanner in the foreword to Wiltshire Village, *which was first published in 1939, '. . . for it is not any one village, but rather an epitome of some of the villages of north-west Wiltshire. The book is to be regarded as fiction rather than as local history; but, like all fiction, it is based on fact.' Heather's prose alongside the etchings and drawings of her late husband, Robin, make* Wiltshire Village *one of the most cherished volumes on any Wiltshire bookshelf. The following passage provides the perfect opening to this anthology since, to use her word, it is the epitome of Christmas in a Wiltshire village between the wars.*

The scarcity of berried holly in the hedges is one of the many signs of the near approach of Christmas. There are more fat geese and turkeys going to Bramelham market; the bus is fuller on Fridays, and the spicy smell of boiling puddings is wafted from the housewives' coppers. There are larger crowds than usual round the butcher's van that calls at Kington Borel on Saturday afternoon. Mrs Coates wants her middle cut of brisket of beef, to be rubbed with black treacle, spices and

saltpetre every day till Christmas Eve, when she will boil it
with the hock in readiness for the visit of her son and his
family. Mrs Gingell has ordered pig's cheek to make into
brawn, and there is a general demand for suet. Dusk has fallen
before the van has finished its round, and it is illuminated
cosily from within. The light falls on the upturned faces of
some dozen children and dogs clustered expectantly at the
open double doors: they are waiting for the women to finish
haggling over the price of backbone, cuttings or shin. At last
it is their turn. The butcher doles them out – children and
dogs alike – a large lump of suet apiece. 'Does 'em good,' he
says. 'Keeps 'em warm.' Too pleased for thanks, the children
run off, sucking their suet as they would a cornet ice, and the
van moves on to Stanley Fitzurse.

Christmas is a busy time for Annie Comely, and the shop is
more crowded than ever. Pink Christmas stockings dangle
from a coloured paper-chain stretched across the already low
ceiling; the inkpot gets mislaid behind the raisins, and there is
only just room among the brown paper parcels and the
home-made plum cakes on the counter for the tray of
Christmas cards, gay with unseasonable roses and pansies and
shiny with embossed celluloid. Sometimes the post office till
runs out of small silver, and some must be borrowed from the
caramel tin containing the shop takings – a procedure
frequently entailing much mental arithmetic, in which the
co-operation of all the waiting customers is sought. But
nothing seems to disturb Mrs Comely's equanimity. She has
been postmistress ever since the death of her mother eighteen
years ago, and even when Mrs Archard was alive Annie helped
whenever she was home; it was she, in fact, who had bought
the letter-box for her mother with her first savings in service:
she had paid two pounds to have it set in the wall beside the
shop window. There were fewer letters to cope with in those
days, but the work was harder, for there was no red mail van,

and the Archard household had to be sorters and postmen combined. Today the van takes letters along the chief roads and Mrs Comely delivers those for the centre of the village while her husband minds the shop; but at Christmas, when the head office at Bramelham needs all the extra help it can get, the village returns to the old way, and the younger Comely children go the long round that used to be their aunt's daily walk.

One old custom that is still kept up here is the singing of the waits on Christmas Eve. They are Tom Coates the sexton and Teacher Miles, who sing bass, Bob Wilkins the mason and Jim Gosling the undertaker, who are tenors, and Daniel Jeffries for the alto parts. Anyone else who accompanies them comes in useful for the verses sung in unison. They sing at three places in the village: at the wellhouse, by the Market Cross, and outside the Manor. When Tom Coates' father was sexton they used to start at midnight, and when they had reached the Manor and had sung 'While shepherds watched,' 'Hark the herald angels sing,' and 'God rest ye merry, gentlemen,' and lastly 'Good Christian men, rejoice,' because that was the old Squire's favourite, he would ask them in and treat them all to mulled ale and mince pies. But Miss Everett does not keep such late hours as her uncle did, and so the waits begin their round earlier. Otherwise the procedure is much the same as it always was.

Though Christmas is more often green than white, winter is not yet over. Sometimes there is hoar frost, when trees are transformed to coral and cobwebs to lace, sometimes snow that is blown and then frozen into sweeping white wings extending from the hedges. Severe weather is far more common after Christmas than before, and seldom does a year pass without a spell of hard frost when the fields are bleached and the ground baked. Moorhens and nuthatches come close to cottage doors in search of food, necessity banishing for the time being their fear of man. In the dark weeks when both earth and water are sealed over, the starling may be seen tunnelling with his beak in the snow for a drink; woodpigeons descend ravenously on the spring cabbages and eat them bare, and the red squirrel, driven by sharp hunger from his hiding-place, gnaws at frozen twigs.

Life is harder even for human beings. The icy east wind blows under cottage doors, where footsteps have worn a hollow in the threshold. Milk freezes in the pail, and neighbours take it in turns to thaw the pumps. But for the children this is all part of the fun. Shepherd's Pond is 'bearing', and they make a slide right across it, following one another shrieking in a long

Skating, or just standing about, on the frozen Kennet and Avon Canal at Devizes, probably during the 1880s

chain. The young men go by moonlight when work is done to the lake in Stanley Park, and play 'hockey' with inverted walking-sticks. Most of them have skates, for although they are not on sale in the Bramelham shops there is usually a pair in the family, acquired so long ago that no one quite knows whose it is. It may be the old-fashioned wooden kind that screws into the heel of the boot; its leather straps may have perished so that it has to be tied on with string; it is probably the wrong size for the present wearer; but there is no time to be fastidious when every available hour is precious right up to the day when the ice creaks ominously and there is an inch of water on the surface. For frosts, the older people say, are not as hard as they were; why, when Emmy Tucker's mother was courting, her young man used to skate all the way from Swindon along the canal to see her.

There is no denying the picturesqueness of 'seasonable' weather. The sun touches the crests of the snow with rose and gold, leaving the hollows violet; the full moon shows the whole landscape uncannily clear, even to the cold white Downs. Now as at no other time the essential shapes of the trees are seen – the neat low hump of the oak, the graceful fans of the elm. Near at hand trunks and branches are bright mossy green where the low afternoon rays strike them; in the distance they are inky blue against the white squares of fields. But this country, wrapped in the sinister silence of frost or seared with bitter winds, is not the beloved familiar scene; alien are the withered grasses rustling like paper, the sky leaden with snow, the ponds in their mask of steely grey. The whole land seems under an interdict. Then suddenly comes the blessed thaw: the air blows soft from the west, the earth yields to the tread, and the first lambs bleat in the fields.

Dull Dark Days

EDITH OLIVIER

*Christmas preparations were rather different if you were a
rector's daughter, and a young lady of sophisticated tastes.
In her autobiography, Edith Olivier, who was born on
New Year's Eve 1872, recalled growing up in Wilton
Rectory, where she lived until 1912. Towards the end of
her life, during which she became the centre of a literary
clique, she was elected the first woman mayor of Wilton.
She died in 1948.*

Our year did not begin on January the first. Ann Thorp, my
grandmother's old maid who lived with us, remarked each year
on the 'dull, dark days before Christmas', and it was in these
dull, dark days that our year began, with Advent Sunday. My
father's preaching turn as a Prebendary of Salisbury often fell
on the Sunday before Advent, and we generally went with him
to the Cathedral Service that afternoon. So the approach of the
new year was heralded for us by the anthem from Mendels-
sohn's 'Lobgesang'.

> Watchman, will the night soon pass?
> The night is departing, depar . . . ting. The day is
> Approaching, approa . . . ching.

The incredible high note was flung into the arches in the pure
fearless tones of the chorister. Each year I still hear in my mind

those soaring notes of confidence in the 'dull, dark days before Christmas'.

Dull and dark they may have been, but they were busy days for us. We were counting the Sunday School marks, and buying the prizes, and then visiting old people to ask what they wanted as Christmas presents. They were always ready for our tap on the door, and had hardly opened it before their own answer rapped out: 'Trowsers', 'Blankets', or 'A dress length'. We noted this down and hastened back into the dull, dark weather. There were our own Christmas presents to make or buy, and we were often rehearsing a play to be performed directly after Christmas. And there were always the church decorations.

They were tremendous in those days. In the broad spaces between the windows were hung large red wooden shields upon which we emblazoned, in holly leaves and dyed everlasting flowers, mysterious ecclesiastical monograms and devices. This meant many pricked and hammered fingers. But the great undertaking each year was making the wreaths of evergreen, for over six hundred yards were required to twine round the pillars and to hang in festoons between them. The only place in Wilton which was big enough for this wreath-making was the Manège at Wilton House, with its sawdust-covered floor, and here we spent about ten days every December. Wooden benches were placed in rows down the length of the Manège, and upon these were laid pieces of rope, some of which were thirty and some forty-five feet long. One end of each piece was fastened to a nail at the end of the bench, and then we sat down and moved slowly backward, as we tied in the pieces of ilex, holly, box, and laurel, of which the festoon was composed. Our teacher was an old gardener, who had done this kind of thing all his life, and he was very strict about our technique. We had to sit 'straddle-legged', and to learn how to graduate the different lengths of stalk in our greenery, so as to make the festoon really strong. It was bitterly cold in the Manège, and round us, as we worked, there rose a cloud of thin dust, made of sawdust and pollen. It always gave me hay-fever, and I sneezed steadily all the time.

Thus described, those dark days before Christmas do indeed sound dull and dark, yet Advent had its heavenly splendour. Those heavy clouds were the right setting for the Advent hymn 'Lo He comes with clouds descending'. And as one thinks oneself back into those days, what emerges most distinctly is the memory of another austerely grand Gregorian tune:

> Rejoice! Rejoice! Emmanuel
> Shall come to thee O Israel.

The short winter days were illuminated by the terror, the majesty, and the joy of the Day of Doom.

For there were many extra services throughout Advent and the hymn-tunes overflowed from the church to the Manège, ringing in our heads as we sneezed among the sawdust.

Soft Weather

MAURICE HEWLETT

At Broad Chalke lived Maurice Hewlett, an accomplished essayist with a legal and civil service background. A keen gardener and countryman, he championed the Wiltshire labourer and served as a magistrate. He also wrote gentle, evocative poetry such as this, published in 1920, three years before his death.

The wind blows mild
Out of the west,
Soft as the lips of a child
On a woman's breast;

And the gray earth
Stirs in her deeps,
In all her intimate valleys
Where the wind creeps,

Sighing in the bents,
Crying beyond,
Ruffling with soft laments
The still dew-pond.

The shepherds are telling
Of open weather
When the ewes and they in the shealing
Must labour together.

· *A Wiltshire Christmas* ·

Come Christmas soon,
With an earth-sigh,
With a blurr'd ring to the moon,
And a mackerel sky;

And Christmas mirth
Stream over the hill,
And peace be yet upon earth
For men of good will!

A frozen trough near Lacock, 1991

Mog

KEN AUSDEN

Ken Ausden was born in Swindon, where he taught until retirement in 1983. He has written plays and two volumes of semi-autobiographical stories about growing up in the railway town just before and during the last war; Up the Crossing *and* Further up the Crossing. *His story-telling has a panache and humour which have won him many admirers, and his work has been broadcast on BBC* Woman's Hour. *Here, as we approach Christmas, is an abridged version of one of his stories; it concerns the delicate problem of getting the present you really want.*

I wanted a cat.

More than anything else in the world, the whole wide world, I wanted a cat. At that particular time!

Even more than I wanted a new pair of foot-ball boots or an Arsenal jersey or a Hornby train set or some ball-bearing roller skates (with spider wheels, of course), I craved a cat.

A cat that I could call my own. I didn't really want someone else to get it for me – though my mother might have done if she had realised how desperate I was – because I didn't want shared ownership. There wasn't any risk of my dad coming up trumps anyway, because he was a dog man and positively detested cats.

So that was all that stood between me and total bliss. Just one small, domesticated, carnivorous quadruped. A moggy!

Christ Church, Swindon, floodlit during the hard winter of
1962–3

'Over my dead body!' was my dad's usual reaction whenever the subject was brought up. 'I'll have no blessed cat in this house. Scratching the furniture, clawing the lino, bringing home fleas and goodness knows what else, digging holes and crapping in me bit of back garden!'

'Please, dad, I won't ever ask for nothin' else as long as I live – honest I won't.'

'I know you of old, me lad. A five minute wonder – that's what it would be.'

'It wouldn't! I'd look after it proper. I'd feed it an' brush it an' teach it to keep out o' your way! An' I'd train it not to scratch nothin' an' not to dig up the garden.'

'Till you get tired of it.' My mother shoved her oar in. 'And then it'll be another job for me.'

'But, mum,' I pleaded. 'I promise—.'

She snuffed out my promise before I could make it. 'How do you propose to feed it, then? With a war on. And rationing. I have job enough to feed you lot without any extra mouths to worry about.'

'I'll get 'is food from the cat meat shop.'

'What are you going to use for money?'

'I'll – I'll get a Saturday job. That'll easy be enough money jus' to feed a little cat. An' I can get fish 'eads for nothin' from Bulgarelli's. An' if I train 'im proper 'e'll eat our left-overs. Ernie Nobes's cat does.'

'And will he get a special milk ration?' asked my dad sarcastically. 'Or d'you know where there's a cow handy so we can get it free!'

Always had the last word, my dad did. Often sarcastic, always final. He was definitely the head of the family (although there were occasions when I had a sneaking suspicion that our mam just let him think he was!).

Time, the great healer of broken dreams, seemed to have lost his first-aid kit, because my flights of fancy grew more

frequent and more urgent as the weeks slipped by. Sometimes I'd get a temporary respite from my yearning, such as when the apple-nogging season arrived, but as soon as life returned to its hum-drum norm, I'd be thinking cats again. Well, not exactly cats – just this one particular cat that I was, one day, going to own.

About a couple of weeks before Christmas mam asked us what we were expecting Father Christmas to bring us for our special present. We always had an Xmas stocking; one of dad's thick, woolly socks clipped to the bed-rail with a clothes peg. And it always had the same things in it. A lump of coal, a sugar mouse, a chocolate watch, a liquorice pipe, an orange, an apple, a packet of sweet cigarettes, a sixpenny tin car/bus/van from Woolie's, two hankies from gran and a couple of little novelties mum would pick up from the Co-op when she went to draw her divi money.

All put there by my dad, creeping in on tip-toe in the early hours of Christmas Day while me and our kid lay there, eyes wide open in the dark, trying not to laugh and spoil dad's Christmas.

But besides the stocking we had one special present. When we were young we made our request in writing and letters addressed to Santa Claus were ceremoniously posted up the chimney. In later years we tossed out verbal suggestions, and while we didn't always get what we asked for, if it was what my mum considered sensible and didn't cost more than about five bob, we stood a fair chance.

'What's it going to be this year, then?' she asked me one afternoon as I was searching through the sideboard drawers for my marble bag. 'Would you like a new satchel to carry your school books instead of that old attache case of your gran's?'

A satchel! For a Christmas present! Swipe me!!

I did something I had not done for ages. I went over to where she was sitting at the kitchen table, darning her way

through the everlasting mountain of socks, and laid my hand on her strong, smooth arm.

'Mam,' I said, giving her the full benefit of anguished, long-suffering look. 'Mam, can I 'ave a kitten?'

She went on with her darning, wriggling the needle in and out of the strands of grey wool, filling in the hole in somebody's heel for the millionth time. I knew she was picking her way among the words she could choose from to give me an answer. I wished I hadn't asked her, hadn't touched her, hadn't made myself look so soft. I wished I was down the rec with Albie. Or up the crossing. Or anywhere but where I was. Waiting.

Mam chucked me under the chin and made me look at her.

'Bad as that, is it?' she asked softly. 'You know what your dad says,' she reminded me, tilting her head and raising her eyebrows.

I nodded.

'He's probably right, you know. Little kittens grow up to be big cats. And a lot of people who love kittens go off them when they grow up. Do you know, a cat can go on to be twenty years old, so I've heard say.'

'Great!' I beamed. ''Cos by that time the war will be over an' I'll 'ave left 'ome an' took the cat with me an' 'e wouldn't be no bother to nobody else an' I could look after 'im in 'is old age!'

There was another of those agonising silences which must have lasted a full half-minute and then mam picked her needle out of the table-cloth, threaded it and drew a fresh sock over her clenched fist. I turned away to resume my search for the lost marble bag, thinking the subject was closed once again, when I heard her give a deep sigh.

'I don't know, I really don't know I'm sure. If only – well, if it wasn't for your dad –.'

So that was it! Only my dad stood between me and my cat. Somewhere in the world – and probably not very far away –

there was a moggy with my name on it, and only my dad prevented me from claiming it. My mother had come off the fence – and landed indisputably on my side.

I retired to the shed down the end of the garden where I did most of my thinking. Not wishing to cause my brain irreparable damage by over-taxing it, I simply allowed myself to drift off on a stream of random ways of infiltrating a cat into our house without falling foul of my dad's strong right arm. The plans varied from the plain unworkable to the extravagantly idiotic.

Until – the first glimmer of inspiration revealed that this was no time for bull-at-a-gate tactics, this required a modicum of skulduggery, an art form at which I had been known to excel. I, obviously, was not the person to introduce the cat into the household. Anyone but me, in fact. And who best of all?

The next several days I was preoccupied with perfecting THE plan and paying twice daily visits to the window of Henson's Super Pet Store. The plan changed shape many times before I was convinced of its infallibility, whilst the objects of my attention in the pet shop window varied from day to day until the afternoon the tabby kitten with a face full of blue eyes appeared. From then on there was no doubt at all. That was my kitten. And the plan had to be made to work.

'Five bob,' said young Bobby Henson. 'And that's a bargain.'

'Five bob!' I scowled. 'That's daylight robbery.'

'That's a quality cat, that is. Not one of your back alley moggies. That cat's nearly got a pedigree!'

I'd heard of dogs with pedigrees, whatever they were, but to have a cat that nearly had one, that would be something special.

'You don't seem to 'ave sold many this week,' I said, staring pointedly at the litter of kittens in the big cage in the window.

'You don't want all them left on your 'ands over Christmas.'

'All right, all right.' Bobby shook his head despairingly. 'I don't know how I make a living out of this, I honestly don't. How about half-a-crown?'

'Great!' I said. ''Ow much a week?'

'Get out of here and stop wasting my time.' I backed off as he made to come round the counter after me.

''Ang on a mo,' I pleaded. 'I want that tabby one, I do reelly. I'll 'ave the money tomorrow. Will you 'ang on to 'im till then? Please?'

Bobby drummed on the till with his fingers while he considered the proposition.

'O.K. then, till this time tomorrow. He's already eating me out of house and home!'

'Thanks, Mr Henson. Give 'im a saucer o' milk from me an' tell 'im I'm comin' for 'im tomorrow.'

Merely the two small obstacles now. When to make the approach for the half-crown and how soon to attempt the infiltration into the house?

'Mum,' I said as she washed up the tea things, the first chance I had to catch her on her own. 'Now I'm more grown up than the other two, could I have the money an' buy my own Christmas present? I've seen what I want an' it's a special offer an' they wouldn't serve anybody else with it 'cept me so d'you think I could 'ave the money to get it tomorrow?'

She carried on rinsing the cups.

'I know you usu'lly spends five shillin's on our big present an' this one what I've seen is only two an' six so you'll be saving two an' six by lettin' me 'ave this one an' I promise I won't ask for nothin' else for Christmas, cross me 'eart an' 'ope to die!'

I did a bit of half-hearted wiping up for her while she mulled over my proposition. After she had emptied the bowl and wiped round the sink, she dried her hands on her apron

and went into the sitting room. I heard her fiddling with the catch on the glass cupboard by the fireplace and my heart did a little somersault in my chest. She came back into the kitchen and held out a half-crown.

'You'll let me see what you've got later on,' was all she said.

'Oh! yes.' I squeezed her fingers as I tried to accept the money graciously rather than avariciously. 'You'll see it later on all right.'

The next evening my dad was doing his good samaritan bit taking old Mr Pinnock from the end house for a Christmas drink at the Gluepot. At five minutes to nine he stepped out of our front door, carefully adjusting the black-out curtain behind him, and very nearly measured his five feet ten inches on the pavement.

'What the hell!' said dad.

'Miaow!' said the kitten.

'Where the devil are you?' Dad felt round his feet in the Stygian darkness as his adversary continued to mew pitifully. He struck a match, cupped his hands around the flame to shield its light from any random jerry aircraft, and discovered the kitten.

He picked it up in one hand and dumped it over the dividing wall into next door's front garden.

'Go home, puss, go on, off with you,' he said, and he didn't sound half as angry as I had feared.

His footsteps played a monotonous, hollow tune on the frosty pavement as he went off down the street, and Albie and me materialised from the shadows.

'Got 'im?' asked Albie.

'Got 'im,' I said, stuffing the furry bundle down the front of my jumper. We nipped down the backs to Albie's shed and restored Mog to his box, a super Co-op grocery box stuffed with shavings from the timber yard.

'It's goin' to work, Albie,' I assured him.

When my dad came home from work at half-past five the following day, Mog was rubbing round his ankles and tugging at his boot laces the second he opened the gate.

'What's this then, puss, you still here?' He lifted the cat and dropped it gently over the fence. Mog caught him up before he reached the back door.

Two minutes later Mog was snuggled down in his cardboard residence enjoying a drop more of Albie's family's milk.

Later that evening, after supper, dad suddenly chucked down the paper and wandered into the back yard. Then he went to the front door and inspected the porch and front garden. He returned muttering to himself about animals taking to certain sorts of people.

Much later when I was in bed, I heard him go to the front door again, and as my dad is a well-balanced man who is not given to talking to himself, I guessed he was enquiring whether there was a little stranger within earshot.

And then it was Saturday. Dad finished work at mid-day. As soon as we'd eaten our scrambled dried egg and chips mum was off into town to collect the butter ration from the Maypole and queue up for whatever was going at the market fish stall. When he finished his after-lunch fag and enough cups of stewed tea to sink the Bismarck, dad appeared in the yard with a roll of gummed brown paper and mum's best scissors and began sticking strips on the window of the outside lav so that if a bomb did land a bit close he wouldn't get showered with flying glass if he was caught on the throne.

I leaned over the wall and dumped Mog on the coal-bunk lid where he proceeded to set up a mournful wail. I waited long enough to see the look on my father's face and for him to pop indoors and reappear with a saucer and a milk bottle. Then I trotted down the street to meet my mother.

We heard him nattering before we opened the gate. When my mother eventually lifted the latch we found him on his

hands and knees chatting up Mog. He looked up at us as guilty as if he'd been caught pinching the crown jewels.

'Well, I mean,' he began lamely and he sounded just like me when I had my back to the wall. 'Three days she's been hanging around here.'

'He,' I corrected him, and wished I hadn't, but no-one seemed to notice.

'Every time I come out she's been here waiting for me. She must have been dead thirsty – she's seen off three saucers of milk! She's a pretty little thing, isn't she? Doesn't belong to anybody round here as far as I can see. Seems to have taken to me, she does.' He got to his feet and dusted off the knees of his trousers. He looked at me – at mum – at the cat – and back to me. 'Here,' he said, 'You're the one who's always on about having a cat. What do you think of this one?'

I picked up Mog.

Dad went indoors.

Mum hesitated on the step and turned to me. 'You'll be wanting a name for that cat, won't you? Why not call it – Half-crown!'

Our eyes met briefly, secretly, as I carried my best ever Christmas present into his new home.

Christmas Pudding and Other Hazards

'The magic of Christmas' leaves a nasty, commercialized, synthetic taste in the mouth nowadays. Was there ever any magic attached to the Wiltshire Christmas? And if there was, did it inspire excitement, wonder, or fear? Magic, remember, along with all kinds of charms, beliefs and superstitions, often wore a terrifying aspect. Here is a ragbag of old customs and beliefs, benevolent and malign, drawn from all over Wiltshire.

The lives of most Wiltshire men and women were bound up with farming, and so it is natural that some of the magic surrounding Christmas should be used to predict and perhaps affect the ensuing year's harvest. A good omen for next year's apple crop was if you could stand under your tree and look at the sun shining through its bare branches on Christmas morning. The phases of the moon around Christmas were an important indicator as well: 'Light Christmas,' ran the proverb, meaning full moon, 'light wheatsheaf; dark Christmas, heavy wheatsheaf'. And here is a rather vague piece of advice (St Stephen's feast is Boxing Day):

'Ere Christmas be passed, let your horse be let blood,
For many a purpose it doth him much good:
The day of St Stephen old fathers did use,
If that do mislike thee, some other day choose.

21

Milton Road, Swindon, after snow in 1908

On the subject of livestock there was a belief well-known in many areas that on Christmas Eve cattle face east and kneel to worship the Christ-child. Various explanations were current to explain why, when put to the test, the animals did not seem to oblige. Perhaps it was the altering of the calendar in 1752, or that the rule only applied to certain cattle – three-year-olds, or seven-year-olds. But it was probably best not to meddle, because at this time of year they could predict the future and had the power of speech. If you overheard them talking it would be bad luck, and they may even foretell your death.

This macabre theme, never far beneath the surface in folk beliefs, showed itself in other ways. If anyone died in the parish over the Christmas period, many more deaths would follow in the coming year. At Seagry, near Chippenham, the belief took a slightly different form. If there was an unburied corpse in the parish on Twelfth Night, then twelve more deaths would ensue. An equally nasty superstition has been found in various places; it claimed that the ghosts of those parishioners who were to die during the coming year could be seen in the church porch on New Year's Eve, by anyone who dared risk seeing themselves or their loved ones.

Even the jovial Christmas pudding, it seems, was lurking there to catch you out. As everyone knew, the day for making it was appointed by the Christian calendar. The 25th Sunday after Trinity (the last before Advent Sunday) was 'Stir-up Sunday'; the collect for that day begins: 'Stir up, we beseech thee, O Lord, the wills of thy faithful people. . . .' For luck, everyone in the household must take part in the stirring; if you missed out, something would happen to you to stop you eating any of it. A wooden spoon must be used (because the manger was wooden), you must wish three times for luck (the Three Wise Men), and stir from east to west (the direction they travelled). A sixpence, a ring and a thimble must be stirred into the mixture, since they would signify wealth, matrimony or 'single-blessedness' to their eventual recipients.

But the proof of the pudding's magic, it seems, was in the eating. 'In January 1894', reported a scholarly clergyman nearly fifty years later, 'Mrs Harris, wife of the Rev Henry Harris, Rector of Winterbourne Bassett, told me the following. A few years ago at the annual choir supper, the clerk was sitting next to Mrs Harris, and when the plum pudding was brought in and put before Mrs Harris, he leant over and said in a low voice, "Don't eat any pudding Mrs Harris". She thought she misunderstood him and when all the company had been helped, everyone of course waiting until she began, as is proper etiquette, she began to eat it, to the clerk's horror. The next day she was taken seriously ill, and the clerk came down to the Rectory and said, "I did all I could to keep her from eating any of that pudding, but she *would* do it, and now she's sure to die". If the Christmas pudding is cracked, the person who first eats of it will have a bad illness and die. The clerk wouldn't eat any of the pudding himself or allow any of his children to eat it.'

But just a minute – Mrs Harris did not die of her illness, did she? She lived to tell the tale. All the same that is quite enough pudding for me, thank you; I shall stick to the mince pies. Especially if there is a sprig of rosemary in the mince-meat, because that will bring good luck. Even better, were I to eat twelve mince pies from twelve separate friends during the twelve days of Christmas, then I should have twelve lucky months ahead of me.

Some Christmas magic is rooted in common sense. Keep the fat from the Christmas goose, for example, because goose grease is an excellent remedy for stiff backs, bruises, and sore udders (on cows). But another remedy smacks more of rank superstition. Not the least interesting aspect is the way in which the information has been preserved. A gentleman from Hull, on Christmas Day 1875, wrote a letter to the *Staffordshire Advertiser*. It was published in the newspaper, and a cutting found its way into a scrapbook kept in the Wiltshire Archaeological Society's Library at Devizes. This is his letter: 'On Christmas Day last year a labourer's wife in Wiltshire came to the clergyman of the parish and asked for a sacrament shilling (i.e., one from the offertory) in exchange for one which she tendered. On enquiry it appeared that her son was subject to fits, and that the only certain remedy was to hang a "sacrament shilling" round the patient's neck. But this must be obtained by first collecting a penny a piece from twelve maidens, then exchanging the pence for an ordinary shilling and then exchanging this shilling for a "sacrament one". This has been tried over and over again, and had never been known to fail except in the case of X where "they hadn't amassed the pence to rights".'

One more thing: be sure to remember to burn all the

Christmas decorations on Candlemas (2 February) – or you never know what might happen.

The Mummers

WILLIAM MORRIS

Mention William Morris in Swindon and it will probably not be the pre-Raphaelite craftsman-socialist who is brought to mind, but the man who founded the town's first newspaper, the Swindon Advertiser *in 1854, and wrote the town's first full-scale history in 1885. He died in 1891. His history describes Swindon on the eve of the railway revolution, and vividly recalls aspects of life quite alien to the town's industrial newcomers. Such as the mummers . . .*

In addition to the out-door sports, there were the in-door amusements, and most notable of all among these were the Mummers, which, forty or fifty years ago, were to be met with in every town and village in North Wilts. During the winter months, up to Christmas Eve. These Mummers, who used to go about from house to house, and more particularly to the public-houses, during the winter evenings, performing a rude kind of play founded on the legend of St George and the Dragon, consisted of six or eight men, who used to wear various kinds of disguises, and who during the season would throw the money they got for their performances into a common fund, which they would distribute at the close of the season *pro ratio* among themselves. Sometimes the company would aspire to nothing more than a recitation set down for each character, but occasionally there would be found a company numbering some ten or twelve persons, including a fiddler, a comic singer, and a dancer, and then the performance would be of a more elaborate character, and the services of the company could only be obtained by a previous engagement, for their 'rounds' were so formed as to include a visit to all the principal residences and farm houses in the neighbourhood. The words of the play performed by these Mummers were partly traditional, and partly local, and were handed down by word of mouth from generation to generation. The plot of the Mummers' play, as I recollect it, was very simple, and quite orthodox. It opened with a general challenge to any knight in Christendom to come forth and dispute some point which was elaborately set forth. The challenge having been accepted, a deadly conflict with swords followed. Fabulous sums of money and everlasting fame were then offered to anyone who should restore the dead knight to life again, which had the effect of bringing forth some wonderful doctor who had a magic pill, one of which being thrust into the mouth of the prostrate body restored animation and the *statu in quo ante*, which consummation was duly celebrated by singing, dancing, and what other forms of rejoicing the company was capable of. As my father was at this time the only bookseller in business in Swindon, I well recollect that every year, just before winter set in, there would be no end of applications for 'Mummer's books'. But these we could never supply, for the simple reason that they were not in existence; and there was therefore no help for it but for those who would play the Mummer's part to get some old Mummer to repeat the words of the several parts over and over again until the learner had got them by heart. Of course, this mode of transmission from the old 'un to the young 'un had its disadvantages. But it had its advantages also, for it admitted of such addition to the dialogue as wit, or fancy, or the circumstances of the times dictated.

Duck's newsagents, Sheep Street, Devizes, in the 1950s. The shop was demolished during the 1960s, and the Post Office now occupies the site

Stourton Customs

E.E. BALCH

*The words of several Wiltshire versions of mummers plays
have in fact survived and been published. This one was
recorded in 1908 from Stourton near Mere; it has several
peculiarities including a character with the somewhat
incongruous name of Doctor Finley. The custom of the
Christmas bull was, as the writer says, very unusual, but
it was not unique to Stourton. It has been reported also
from Dorset, and from Kingscote near Dursley in Gloucestershire.*

A Wiltshire village, six miles from the nearest railway station,
and so hidden from the high-road that few motorists discover
it, might be thought safe from the incoming tide of modern
innovation. And outwardly, indeed, Stourton has changed
very little since Hazlitt wrote of it nearly seventy years ago:

'After passing the park-gate, which is a beautiful and
venerable relic, you descend into Stourton by a sharp winding
declivity, almost like going underground, between high
hedges of laurel trees, and with an expanse of woods and water
spread beneath.

'It is a sort of rural Herculaneum, a subterranean retreat.
The inn is like a modernized guard-house; the village church
stands on a lawn without any enclosure; a row of cottages
facing it, with their whitewashed walls and flaunting honey-
suckles, are neatness itself. Everything has an air of elegance,
and yet tells a tale of other times. It is a place that might be

held sacred to stillness and solitary musing!'

Yet old customs disappear rapidly even here; and with the dust of ignorance and folly are swept away some better things. Not to be regretted least is the spirit which was not ashamed to play; which found its pleasure among its neighbours, and at its own door, before the age of cheap excursions and entertainments. Amateur theatricals and penny readings are doubtless excellent, yet one may question whether the old mumming play did not make for more simple and genuine merriment. This play was handed on by word of mouth, never, I think, written; and the small company of actors guarded their rights jealously. There were seven characters: Father Christmas, the Duke and Duchess of Northumberland, Captain Curly from the Isle of Wight, Doctor Finley, Johnnie Jack, and Bighead, or 'Girthead'.

Father Christmas acted the part of the chorus, opening with a speech in which he hinted broadly at the wishes of the mummers:

> I hope your pocket is full of money.
> And I hope your cellar is full of beer,
> And I hope I shall get a little
>   'fore I go from here.

The characters entered one by one, and each introduced the next by the invitation, 'So walk in, —!'.

The Duchess was a lady of domesticated habits, singularly free from pride of rank, for she entered next, carrying a broom:

Here comes I, Miss Duchess, with my broom, broom, broom,
To sweep the room clean for the Duke and the Captain to
    have room for to fight.

The part was of course taken by a boy, resplendent in a

long-trained dress. The fight followed on a truculent dialogue between the Duke and Captain Curly. (One wonders what principle of selection determined the localities from which these gentlemen arrived. Were Northumberland and the Isle of Wight the most remote which readily occurred to the mummers?)

> *DUKE*: Here is the Duke, the Duke of Northumberland,
> With my broad sword in hand.
> Where is the man? I bid him stand.
> I'll cut him in humerus, and as small as a fly;
> I'll send him to the cook-shop for to make mince-pie.
> So walk in, Captain.
> *CAPTAIN*: Here comes the Captain, Captain Curly!
> Duke, I heard your voice from out the chimney.
> *DUKE*: Pray, what did you hear, Captain Curly?
> *CAPTAIN*: I heard the challenge of Captain Curly.
> Here comes I, so light as a fly;
> But I've no money, but what cares I!
> Here comes I from the Isle of Wight,
> Unto the Duke of Northumberland;
> Here comes I to fight.
> So mind yourself, and guard your blows;
> Off comes your head, if not your nose!

After the Duke has been wounded, and duly dosed by Doctor Finley, there entered the most interesting character – the most interesting because the least obvious – Johnnie Jack. He carried a number of small dolls on his back:

> Here comes I, little Johnnie Jack,
> With my wife and family at my back.
> My wife's so big, my family's so small,
> If I hadn't come when I had

I'd have starved them all.
Out of five I saved but one;
All the rest is dead and gone.
So, ladies and gentlemen, have pity on me,
Poor Johnnie Jack, and his great wife and he.

No amount of questioning elicits any explanation of the
origin of this character, or of the dolls at his back; but behind
the burlesque figure and the doggerel lines there surely lurks
the dim hero of some forgotten legend.

Lastly comes Bighead:

Here comes I, that's never been yet,
With my big head, and little wit.
My head's so big, my wit's so small,
I've brought my fiddle to please you all.

And the mumming ended in a country dance. The humour
throughout was of the broadest description – as, for instance,
the cry of Captain Curly:

The Duke is wounded to his heart.
Five hundred pounds I *wouldn't* put down
If a noble doctor can be found.

Or the claim of the doctor:

DOCTOR: I'll cure the hickly, pickly, palsy, or the gout.
I'll cure old Jack Daw with the toothache,
Or old Mag-Pie with the headache.
CAPTAIN: Pray, how do you that, Mr Finley?
DOCTOR: By twisting their heads off, and sending their bodies
into ditch.

Proof of the antiquity of the play is to be found in the presence of some words which have been mangled till they have lost all meaning, but which are faithfully repeated. Thus the Duke: 'I'll cut him into *humerus*'.

Quite distinct from the mummers, though also coming on Christmas Eve, was the Christmas bull. The head of a bull with great bottle eyes, large horns, and lolling tongue, was manipulated by a man stooping inside a body composed of a broomstick, a hide of sacking and a rope tail. The bull knocked at the door with its horns, and, if allowed to enter, chased the young people round the house, with fearsome curvets and bellowings. Even in the surrounding parishes the Christmas bull is unknown, and I have never heard of the custom being practised in other parts of the country. The man in whose possession the bull was until quite recently, knows that it has been in his family for over one hundred years. It was used till about ten years ago.

On Old Christmas Eve came the wassailers with their traditional song:

> Wassail, wassail!
> All round the town!
> Your cup is so white,
> And your beer is so brown.
>
> Missus and master,
> Now we are come here,
> Give us a cup
> Of your best Christmas beer.
>
> *CHORUS*
> For it's our wassail,
> And a jolly wassail,
> And joy be to you,
> For it's our wassail.

· A Wiltshire Christmas ·

Pretty little maiden,
With your silver lace,
Open wide your hall-doors
And show us your face.

Pretty little maiden,
With your silver pin,
Open wide your hall-doors
And let us all in.

Missus and master,
A-sitting by the fire,
And we poor sinners
A-dabbing in the mire.

Missus and master,
If you be so willing,
Send out your youngest son
With the round shilling.

Missus and master,
We must be gone,
God bless you all
Till we come again!

The wassailing serves as a link between the jollities connected with Christmas and those which cluster round the
agricultural festivals; though the custom of wassailing the
apple-trees, which, I believe, survives in Devonshire, has
disappeared here. Hardy, rough, and hearty were the men who
used to sing such songs as these. A softer generation may well
listen to the stories they can tell before they altogether sink
into silence.

The Cricklade Wassail

ALFRED WILLIAMS

Wiltshire's best known collector of folk songs and folklore, Alfred Williams, recorded as many details as possible of the Cricklade wassail before the custom disappeared. Williams, poet and self-taught polymath, lived at South Marston and worked in Swindon railway factory, an experience which he described in a famous book published in 1915. Here is a seasonal contribution which he wrote for a local newspaper, the North Wilts. Herald, *in 1928, just over a year before his death.*

We get the best evidence of the local Wassail from the Cricklade practice, particulars of which I obtained of an old man by the name of Harvey, who died in 1916, at the age of ninety. He was called 'Wassail' Harvey, because he was the last survivor of the Cricklade wassailers. His father and grandfather had also been members of the wassail team. From him I learned full details of the local wassail as it was practised in his day; it had been discontinued for about half a century.

The principal feature of the Cricklade wassail was the employment of the ox. Herein we have a clue to the exact significance of the wassail, which was not merely a drinking of healths, but a ceremony performed in order to obtain fertility of crops, and the prosperity of flocks and herds. It was only an effigy that figured in the rite in later years; but earlier it was a live animal. In this we may see the gradual decay of the ceremony. The change from the live beast to the effigy was the first step – faith in the efficacy of the rite had waned, and the husbandman no longer lent his ox to walk in the procession. But popular enthusiasm kept the custom going for a time, until, we may suppose, the cool reception given to the wassailers quenched their ardour. If no gifts were forthcoming, and if the bowl were not filled, there would be no procession, and no song. The fact is that wassailing, as a popular custom, had become unprofitable.

The effigy of the ox was made of a withy frame, with a cured hide, having the ears, horns and tail intact, stretched over it. The fore-parts were stuffed with straw; and for eyes two small red lamps were fixed inside the head. When Christmas arrived, and the mummers and carol-singers began to go their rounds, the wassailers turned out and formed their procession. Two of the sturdiest among them crept into the hollow figure and bore it along on their backs, imitating the swaying motion of the animal. When the spectators pressed too near the ox was made to swish its tail. This kept a clear space for the wassailers, and provided amusement for the crowd.

The chief wassailer walked in front of the ox, carrying the time-honoured bowl, which was made of wood, and decorated with holly and mistletoe. The remainder of the company followed, dressed in fancy costumes, and wearing streamers and ribbons. They visited the farmhouses and the dwellings of the bettermost people, and sang the song – 'Wassail, wassail, all over the town', etc. In the course of the piece the ox was fully toasted – first his horn, then his eye, ear and tail. Afterwards the master and mistress were addressed, and prosperity invoked in the shape of good crops of hay and corn – exactly in keeping with the pagan custom. At the conclusion of the song the maid, or the mistress of the house, brought warm spiced ale, whiskey or punch, with toast and roasted apples, and filled the bowl. She also pinned ribbons to the dresses of the wassailers, which were kept as trophies.

The Boy Bishop of Salisbury

One of the most popular attractions in Salisbury Cathedral is the medieval clock. Its mysterious workings near the west end of the north aisle are often surrounded by admirers. Behind them as they inspect its crude horology, between two pillars of the nave arcade, there has reposed the stone effigy of a bishop, ever since it was removed there early in the seventeenth century. Nothing remarkable about that, perhaps, except that he is less than three feet tall. The likely explanation, first offered in 1811, is that the sculpture covers not the whole body of a bishop, but the buried heart, entrails or some other portion of his anatomy, and that the rest of him lies elsewhere. But when the monument was first discovered and placed there, possibly in about 1616, this was not realized, and by 1649 a completely different explanation had gained currency. It referred back to a custom, discontinued for a century, of electing each Christmas from among the choristers a 'boy-bishop', who, for a few days each year, was treated with all the

The medieval tomb in Salisbury Cathedral, which was once
thought to commemorate a boy bishop

respect accorded to, and carried out many of the duties
performed by, the real bishop at other times. The tomb, so the
story ran, must have commemorated one such boy bishop who
died during his brief tenure of office.

This strange custom of the boy bishop, by no means
restricted to Salisbury, but practised in many medieval
cathedrals and parish churches, was older than Salisbury
Cathedral itself. Indeed it was in a sense older even than
Christianity, because it has a close affinity with the Roman
festival of Saturnalia, held at the same time of year, when
servants dressed up as their masters and were waited on by
them, and everything was topsy-turvy. It had links too with
other pagan and Christian midwinter festivals. In the Church
calendar 28 December is Holy Innocents' Day or Childermas,
commemorating Herod's infanticide, and this quite naturally
became the feast around which the boy bishop's activities were

centred. In some churches his election took place three weeks earlier, on 6 December. This was the feast of St Nicholas (Santa Claus), the patron saint of children, whose cult became extremely popular around 1100. Also around Christmas the Lord of Misrule and the Feast of Fools offered excuses for thinly disguised pagan festivities in the Saturnalian tradition.

The boy bishop was a cathedral chorister, and was elected by his fellow-choristers, who jealously guarded their right to choose him themselves. Special vestments were provided for his use, and with his fellows he took the place of the real bishop and senior clergy at the cathedral services from vespers on 27 December (the feast of St John the Evangelist) until vespers on the following day, Holy Innocents'. During this time the senior clergy took on the role of the choristers, occupying the lower stalls and performing the humbler duties. Although he did not actually officiate at mass on Holy Innocents' Day, the boy bishop did preach the sermon. It would have been written for him to deliver, and generally dealt with the topic of childhood. As his reward for these rather awe-inspiring responsibilities he was allowed to pocket the offerings (known as oblations) made at the high altar on that day; these could amount to a handsome sum by medieval standards, exceeding £5 on at least one occasion.

If from this description you have a picture of angelic choirboys solemnly performing an ancient ritual you would probably be quite wrong. There survive from medieval Salisbury enough prohibitions, and reports of 'manifest unruliness' surrounding the proceedings, to suggest that, in the spirit of Saturnalia, this was a time for letting off steam, mocking all authority, and generally messing about. On one occasion, in 1448, high spirits turned to tragedy. The choristers, returning home from a supper-party at a canon's house, became involved in a fight with a ribald crowd of unruly vicars, one of whom mortally wounded a servant of the canon. After that misfortune a strict rule was enforced that vicars should not carry weapons except under special circumstances.

The ceremony of the boy bishop lasted as long as the Middle Ages, but it could not survive the strictures of the Reformation. In 1541 a royal proclamation forbad all such 'dyvers and many superstitions and chyldysh observances', in which 'children be strangelie decked and apparayled to counterfeit priestes, bishoppes, and women, and so be led with songs and daunces from house to house, blessing the people and gatheryng of money; and boyes do singe masse and preache in the pulpitt, with suche other unfittinge and inconvenient usages'.

And so the practice died, and Salisbury forgot all about it, except for the effigy in the cathedral nave – and that refers to something else altogether.

A Party to Remember

CECIL BEATON

Perhaps the spirit of the strange medieval custom of the boy bishop lives on in the attempts by important grown-ups to entertain children at Christmas. Here is a bemused Cecil Beaton, invited to a children's party in 1931 at Ferne House, near Donhead. Beaton then lived nearby, at Ashcombe, and recorded the incident in his volume of diaries, The Wandering Years, *which was published in 1961.*

At last we found ourselves marshalled into the drawing-room, where a spindly Christmas tree stood decorated with tinsel toys and illuminated by coloured bulbs. Soon the village children from Berwick St John trooped in by invitation – fifty or sixty of them standing like a military unit. They had large heads, pale, weedy complexions, and goggle eyes. An overfat schoolmaster, crimson in the face, conducted a hymn while his minions sang with only a remote interest in the proceedings.

The Duchess stood to attention surrounded by many ugly, grey-haired women, including a few deaf mutes. The village children, puny and unattractive, made a startling contrast to the healthy ducal offspring.

Her Grace then spoke a few words, welcoming the local

children and giving them a dissertation on the advantages of country over city. Each leaf, she explained, was different in the country. There were many things to watch; they must appreciate and preserve its rustic joys.

One boy was asked the main difference between town and country and ruggedly replied, 'Oi think the moine difference is that in the cities there is so much dust and doirt and muck. In the country, the air is different and there are flewers.'

'Quite right, that is excellent.' The Duchess seemed a stalking crane in her off-white flannel skirt, socks and gym shoes. Finally she excoriated those who are cruel to the animals. 'Above all you must be kind to birds.'

The children were then encouraged to give bird calls for Father Christmas. They moved joylessly into the pitchpine panelled hall and intoned at the top of their melancholy screechy voices. After delays, and hitches and whispered commands from the family, and repeated shouts in unison from the children, Father Christmas materialised in the form of the Duke who was wheeled on to the scene by Geordie, his stalwart son. The Duke was dressed in red flannel with hood and a wig of white cotton wool. The children were told to line up in order of their ages. Those who were twelve years old must head the procession and be given a present.

A few mumbled words, then the village children were given orders to troop as a platoon into the frigid drawing-room. Each child took an orange and an apple from fruit-filled Tate sugar boxes placed near the door.

Everyone waited: grey-haired women, deaf mutes, refugee cats and dogs, and children of all ages. Then the lights went out; a few of the smaller village children began to whimper. The ducal grandchildren crawled in and out of legs, human and animal, while outside the French windows their handsome parents could be seen for a flash or two, as they ran in the stormy darkness with matches and beacons. Suddenly a

Catherine wheel hissed; then in the rain appeared a shower of 'golden rain'; squibs popped; jumping crackers exploded on the wet ground; chinese crackers went off in a series of half-hearted reports.

The whimpering village children now burst into screams of alarm. Terrified of the darkness and the noise, they howled, bellowed, shrieked with each new explosion. Babies cried, dogs barked, oranges and apples rolled on the floor. From exploding rockets blinding flashes revealed a maggot-crawling mass of panicking children and dogs. The hysteria reached a terrifying crescendo when a spurting, spluttering 'sparkler' came flying indoors.

Evaporated Apricots and Plain Grosvenor

Until it closed a few years ago the grocery and provisions shop of Messrs Wilson & Kennard at 14 Market Place, Warminster was an important and well-respected part of the town's commercial life. It had been trading since the turn of the century, and for a few years before that, until Jimmy Kennard came on the scene, it was Wilson &

Mayo's. A 1900 advertisement lists the firm's specialities: 'Finest Stilton Cheese (rich, ripe, and blue), direct from the Dairies in Leicestershire; Bass's Ale and Guinness's Stout in brilliant condition; Exceptionally fine Devonshire Cider in Bottles; Importers of Tarragona direct (specially recommended)'. Their mouthwatering Christmas Catalogue, probably dating from around the same time, runs as follows:

Wilson & Mayo beg to intimate that they have just completed their purchase of FANCY and other GOODS, suitable for Christmas Trade, the quality of each article being the very best obtainable. The Goods will be Displayed on a Stand, inside

A magnificent display for Christmas outside a Swindon butchers in about 1910. The shop stood near the corner of Fleet Street and Bridge Street

the Shop, from December 14th, and the favour of your kind inspection is requested at an early date.

Bonbons: a large and varied stock from 6d to 2s 6d per box.

Dessert Fruits: French Plums in 2lb and 4lb boxes (loose 6d per lb); Elvas Plums, 2lb boxes; Tunis Dates, 1lb and 2lb fancy carton; Taffilat Dates, very choice (cheaper qualities at 3d per lb); finest pulled Figs, 2lb boxes; finest layer Figs, 1lb and 2lb boxes; cooking Figs, 3d and 4d per lb; Muscatells, choicest quality 1s 3d per lb, special value 1s per lb, good quality 10d per lb; Metz Fruits, in $\frac{1}{4}$lb, $\frac{1}{2}$lb, 1lb and 2lb fancy boxes; also Crystallized Angelica, Apricots, Cherries, Chinois, Ginger, and Glacée Cherries.

Huntley and Palmer's Specialities: Cakes: Iced Almond, Chatsworth, Fruit, Marlborough, Mairfair [*sic*], Balmoral, Novelty, Rutland; Plain Grosvenor, Royal, Fruit, Genoa, Madeira, Bristol, Sandringham, Lisbon, Eton, Palace; Biscuits: a very handsome selection of fancy tins in all shapes and sizes.

Nuts: Black Spanish, Barcelona, Brazils, Shell Almonds, Chesnuts [*sic*], Wallnuts [*sic*].

Oranges, Lemons, Apples, Grapes, Normandy Pippins, Evaporated Apricots, etc, etc.

Wine, Spirit, & Beer Department: Spirits: all are well matured and the age is from five to eight years, no new qualities kept in stock. Wines: a large stock of very choice qualities, including a few special lines as under: Tarragona (our importation), 1/6 quart bottle; Pale Sherry, 15/–, 18/–, 20/– per dozen; Choice Port, 24/–, 30/–, 36/– per dozen; Claret (1893 vintage), 18/–, 20/– per dozen; Bass's Best Pale Ale, imperial half pint and pint bottles; Bass's Light Table Ale, imperial pint bottles; Imperial Ale (speciality 2/– dozen) pint bottles; Guinness's Stout, imperial half pint and pint bottles.

Provisions: Choice Blue Stiltons direct from Dairies in

Leicestershire; Choicest Gorgonzolas; Choicest Cheddars; Choice Somersets; Very Fine Truckles.

Bacon: Prime Wiltshire, smoked or plain; Choicest Irish Smoked Hams; Own-Cured Plain Hams and Bacons.

Pork Pies: our own make, already noted throughout the town and neighbourhood.

Please order requirement for Christmas a week beforehand.

Tha Girt Big Figgetty Pooden

EDWARD SLOW

Edward Slow's dialect verse was aimed at ordinary Wiltshire men and women. He was a carriage-builder in Wilton, where he was born in 1841; he took inordinate pride in his little town, and rose to be its mayor in 1892 and 1905. Edith Olivier knew him, and described him in her autobiography as 'the last of the old minstrels'. For much of his life he published poems, tales, anecdotes and eventually a novel in Wiltshire dialect. The poems appeared between 1867 and 1898, and a collected edition was published in 1903. This is one of his most popular pieces — the opening lines were even incorporated into the Shrewton mummers play.

· A Wiltshire Christmas ·

Ah, wen I wur a girt hard bwoy,
We appetite nar mossel coy,
Tha baste thing out ta gie I joy
   Wur a girt big figgetty pooden.

Tha very neam ow'un zeem'd anuff
An ta smill un, ow did meak I puff,
An lor, ow I did vill an stuff,
   When mother mead a pooden.

Hache birthday she wur sure ta meak,
A girt plum pooden, an a keak,
An ax a vew vrens to parteak,
   Of her nice figgetty pooden.

Tho mother adden much ta spend
She mead un good ya may depend,
An purty quick ther wur a end,
   A thick ar birthday pooden.

Na vear a any on't getten stale,
If I wur handy an wur hale,
Me appetite hood never vail,
   As long as ther wur pooden.

Not that I wur a girt big glutton
Like thic chap, as ate a laig a mutton,
Tho me waiscut oft I did unbutton
   When twur a extry girt un.

When I wur in tha village choir,
An a veast wur gied ess be tha Squire,
Tha us'd ta com in ael a vire,
   An as black mwoast as me hat.

· *A Wiltshire Christmas* ·

A vignette illustration to accompany this poem, published in
Edward Slow's 1903 edition of his collected verse

An twur rare vun to zee em smoke,
Var in wine an brandy they did zoak,
An pon me zong it wur no joke,
    Aten much a that ar pooden.

Var mezelf I'd zooner av em plain,
Zo's you can cut an com again,
Wieout tha dread a gien ee pain,
    Like tha there brandy poodens.

Wen in ta Zalsbry oft I went,
Var measter on a errant zent,
I warn, mwoast ael me brass wur spent,
    In buyin zim figgetty pooden.

· A Wiltshire Christmas ·

I used ta knaa a leetle shop,
In Brown Street, wur I off did pop,
An well vill up me ungry crop,
    We nice sweet figgetty pooden.

Tha used ta beak em in a tin.
An tha ooman she did offen grin,
Ta zee ow zoon I did ate in
    Her nice hot figgetty pooden.

Times on times we vun she've cried,
An wur ablidged ta hould her zide,
Ta zee ow zoon away I'd hide,
    That ar dree penneth a pooden.

It done her good she did declare,
Ta zee I ate me pooden there,
An she aelways gied I mwourn me shear,
    Cos I wur vond a pooden.

Ah, oft I thinks apon tha time,
When Crismis bells merry da chime,
What a girt pooden, nice an prime,
    Mother did meak var we.

A used ta come in steamin hot,
Nearly as big's a waishen pot.
Wie vigs an currands zich a lot,
    In thick ar Crismis pooden.

Lore, ow me young eyes glissen'd at un,
An fiather he did zay, 'Odd drat 'un,'
I do believe while I wur chatten,
    Thic bwoy ud ate thic pooden.

48

The Philips family of Salisbury celebrating Christmas together
in their terraced house in Sidney Street, 1936/7

Dree sorrens on't I aelwys had,
An fiather he did look like mad,
Bit mother she wur aelwys glad,
    An zay 'Lar let'n av his pooden.'

A coose, I diden av much mate,
Nar gierden stuff apon me plate,
An pooden aelwys wur a trate,
    Specily thick one at Crismis.

Tho I own, I did av mworn me wack,
Me lips var mwore did offen smack,
An we waistcut offen wur main slack,
    Wen tha pooden wur ael gone.

· A Wiltshire Christmas ·

His mother once mead a girt pooden,
Thinkin she'd gie her bwoy a dooin;
Atter aten till na mwore a cooden,
   Cry'd, cos a adden vinish'd un.

Wen I grow'd up a biggish bwoy,
Wat thay calls a hobbledehoy,
Tha chaps did try I to annoy
   Be caalin out 'Figgetty pooden.'

Bit there I diden use ta keer,
Var ael ther chaff, an joke, an sneer,
I diden stop it, never vear,
   Wen ther wur any pooden.

A contented bwoy I aelways wur,
An diden cry an meak a stur,
Wen he wur gone cos there wurnt mwore,
   Like a bwoy I knaas who did.

If ever I da av a wife,
Ta liv wie I ael droo thease life,
I'll tell her, if she dwoant want strife,
   Ta meak I plenty a poodens.

Begar, I hooden mind betten a crown,
That if a chap is mainly down,
Nuthen ull cure un I'll be bown,
   Like a girt big figgetty pooden.

A zeems ta drave ael keer away,
An meak yer heart veel light an gay,
That you'll zeem merry ael tha day
   Atter aten figgetty pooden.

· A Wiltshire Christmas ·

Zoo teak thease hint ael labourers wives
If you da wish var happy lives,
You'll av em zure, if you contrives
   Ta get lots a figgetty poodens.

If ya caant avoord much butcher's mate,
Ta putt apon yer husbin's plate,
Putt avore un then, what he can ate,
   A nice girt figgetty pooden.

His health an straingth it will zustain,
An vlesh he's zartin zure to gain,
An a unger never he'll complain,
   If ya gets un lots a pooden.

Meself, ael things I hood gie up,
Even do wieout me pipe an cup,
Var I cud dinner, tay, an zup,
   On a nice girt figgetty pooden.

A Christmas cake weighing 120 lb which was baked at George
Rouse's bakery in Castle Street, Salisbury in 1907, to be cut
up and sold in the shop

52

The Grand-Master's Dinner

MICHAEL BURROUGH

The author of this gastronomic extravaganza was a Salisbury banker. He was mayor of the city in 1790, his bank failed in 1810, and he died in 1831. A manuscript volume of his poems, a commonplace book and some other personal effects have been preserved among the papers of his executor, and are now in the Wiltshire Record Office. So far as I am aware none of his poetry has been published before. The following work will be of greater interest to students of menus than of literature.

At Christmas it is such a rare jolly time,
With eating and drinking, while yet in our prime;
If I was made king, to my subjects I'll swear,
That Christmas should last for the whole of the year.
There's another good reason why Christmas should last,
Such a season for feasting should never be past;
In mirth and in good fellowship I take great delight up
With singing and music for to keep the night up
I'll now give you an account of our Grand-Master's dinner,
It is true what I say, although I'm a sinner.
How brought on the table, on last Christmas Day,
And how it went off, I am going to say.

· A Wiltshire Christmas ·

But first I should rather say how it came on,
A turbot at top, which was very well done;
Boiled turkey at bottom, with rich oyster sauce,
And forcemeat balls round it all fried to a toss.
A chine was placed near, t'other end was a ham,
And a piece of roast beef, on which you might cram.
Chickens roasted and boiled, at the sides in array,
Such nice ones you'll be sure could not hope for fair play.
There was also a tongue, and hash calves-heads and brains,
But to mention each dish I need take no more pains.
Suffice there was plenty, and that of the best,
Then a haunch of fat venison, to crown all the rest.
The set to then began, with great skill from the first of it,
The meat was cut up, and of course had the worst of it.
The turkey and fowls of their limbs were bereft
And the venison and beef cut in right and left.
Not the meats, but the men, who attacked it were tough,
And the battle long lasted, e'er one cried enough.
Such eating and drinking there was on that day,
Each took what he liked, and drank his own way.
Now the cloth being drawn, soon the wine glasses rattle,
Which succeeded the noise of the knife and fork battle.
All drank what they liked, whether old port or sherry,
And toasted away, until all was quite merry.
A bumper filled and all ready, then up rose the host,
And proposed to his friends he saw round him, a toast
With three cheers, which he knew would make the room
   ring
With a hearty good will, 'Twas Great George our King.

One Person, Drinking

MAUD DAVIES

We know more about the parish of Corsley at the beginning of the twentieth century than anywhere else in Wiltshire. But we know rather less about the life and tragic death of our informant. Maud Davies studied at the London School of Economics under Sydney and Beatrice Webb, who suggested that she should investigate the sociology of her own village. The resulting book, Life in an English Village, *was published in 1909. Miss Davies then moved to London, where she studied poverty and became involved in philanthropic causes. But in February 1913 her body was found on a railway line near Kensington and, although an open verdict was recorded, she was thought to have taken her own life. She was thirty-seven. Here she describes the community's drinking habits at Christmas.*

Social life in Corsley centres round the family or household, round clubs for games and recreation, and the public-houses, and round the churches or chapels of the various religious denominations. In a scattered parish, such as Corsley, where many of the houses are situated in lonely lanes, the family is naturally inclined to live a more isolated life than in villages where even on a dark winter's night the street forms a sociable meeting-place; and although Corsley is well provided with public-houses – and it cannot be said that these are unattended – yet most of the married men prefer to have their cask of beer at home, taking a glass after supper with their wives, rather than turn out habitually into the dark muddy lanes which have to be traversed before they reach the haunts of men.

When inquiries as to the population were being made during the winter of 1905–6, many of the visits were paid between 6 and 7.30 pm. At this time the whole family would almost invariably be found at home, grouped round the fire, or where there were children they might be seated round the table playing some game. At Christmas-time not uncommonly a small Christmas-tree for the children would be standing in the corner of the room. A large proportion of the young people of Corsley quit the parish on leaving school; but the young men who remain very frequently take up some hobby, such as fretwork, photography or music, with which they employ their evenings quite happily at home. The few young girls who stay with their parents usually complain that it is 'dull', especially in the winter, when they often go out very little. These remarks naturally apply more to the smaller hamlets of Corsley than to Chapmanslade, where a real village exists, with a somewhat different type of social life, and where the parishioners of Corsley join with those of Westbury, on the other side of the way, in getting up concerts, dances, and other festivities during the winter months. Music is the fashion here, too, and Chapmanslade has its own brass band, composed of local musicians.

But even in other parts of Corsley a few occasions for social gathering occur in the course of the winter. Of late years most successful and popular dramatic entertainments have been given at the school by the children of the parish, under the tuition of the master and mistress. Occasionally, too, a concert is got up at the reading-room. Such entertainments are always largely attended.

Evening services at the chapels take out some of the older people, and there is probably a little visiting of each other in the evening among the more well-to-do.

But while part of the people appear to be almost puritanical in their lives, it must be admitted that there are some families who regularly frequent the public-house. It is not the custom for sons living at home to pay more than 7s or 8s per week to their parents, unless in exceptional cases. A few sons living with parents consequently get into the habit of working only part time, and thus take to loafing ways, working on odd jobs not more than two or three days a week, much to the distress of the parents. Those young men who, working regularly, occupy their leisure with performance on a musical instrument, or some such hobby, usually save a good deal of money. Others, though spending a considerable part of their earnings on beer and tobacco, yet manage to save something. A remaining section spend all they get on food and drink, or dissipation in the neighbouring towns, to the neglect sometimes of their recognised liabilities to relatives. These people, mostly unmarried men, described by a native of Corsley as 'sillylike', thinking, she says, of nothing but what they eat and drink, and going to the public-house in the evening for a 'lark', form the chief clientele of the public-houses. It was not found possible to ascertain the amount of beer consumed in Corsley, for while some keepers of public-houses were good enough to furnish particulars, others declined to do so, and a large amount of beer is also taken direct from the brewers by the cottagers and others. It cannot, however, be doubted that the average consumption per head is somewhat large. At Christmas-time, 1905, notes were made of persons in the six public-houses of Corsley, including one situated a few yards outside the parish, with the following results:

December 25th Present
1. 9 pm.   8 men, 2 wives.
2. 9.30 pm. 11 men, 4 strange women. Singing.
3. 9.50 pm. 13 men, 1 wife, also 10 strangers, male and female. Gramophone and singing.

December 26th
1. 7.30 pm. 15 men.
2. 8 pm.   17 men.
3. 8.30 pm. 17 men, with 5 wives or daughters, 4 strangers, male and female. Gramophone.

December 27th
1. 9 pm.   10 men.
2. 10 pm.   5 men, one with wife and daughter from Frome.
3. 9.30 pm. 14 men. Concertina and tambourine playing.
4. 8.15 pm. 6 persons. Talking of coming election.
5. 9 pm.   4 persons. Talking about Ireland, one of the company being bound there.
6. 7.45 pm. 4 persons. Playing bagatelle.

December 28th
1. 9.30 pm. 8 men.
2. 9.30 pm. 8 men.
3. 6 pm.   9 men.
4. 8 pm.   7 persons. Talking of agriculture.
5. 7 pm.   2 persons. Playing darts.
6. 9 pm.   6 persons. Playing bagatelle.

December 29th
4. 9 pm.   5 persons. Playing darts.
5. 9.30 pm. 1 person. Drinking.
6. 9 pm.   6 persons. Playing bagatelle.

December 30th

1. 7 pm.   4 men.
2. 7.30 pm.   2 men. The landlord gave free drinks, 8.30 to
               10 pm., to finish up the Christmas holidays.
3. 8 pm.   5 men.

December 31st

1. 9 pm.   8 men.
2. 8 pm.   9 men.
3. 9.40 pm.   6 men.

January 1st

4. 9.30 pm.   3 persons. Playing darts.
5. 8 pm.   8 persons. Playing darts.
6. 8.30 pm.   2 persons. Drinking only.

January 2nd

4. 9 pm.   1 person. Drinking.
5. 9.45 pm.   2 persons. Playing darts.
6. 9.15 pm.   4 persons. Playing bagatelle.

January 3rd

4. 8.45 pm.   10 persons. Talking of the coming election.
5. 8 pm.   4 persons. Playing dominoes.
6. 9.15 pm.   8 persons. Playing bagatelle and talking of the
               coming election.

January 6th

4. 8.30 pm.   5 persons. Talking of shooting pigeons, there
               being a shooting match in the village.
5. 8 pm.   10 persons. Playing darts and talking of
               coming election.
6. 9 pm.   9 persons. Playing bagatelle – some only
               drinking.

It is not to be supposed that this census, taken at Christmas-time, and when also an election was looming in the near future, is in any way typical of the ordinary attendance, which is probably considerably smaller at a less festive season. Moreover, besides the number of persons noted as 'strangers', many names are included of persons not residing in Corsley, though well known to some of the inhabitants. An investigation at this time, however, showed the kind of amusement which was sought in these houses, games such as 'darts' or bagatelle probably taking an even more prominent place at a season when exceptional entertainments such as gramophones and singing were unprovided. But no doubt, though the number who go merely to 'soak' may not be numerous, a considerable amount of liquor is consumed by the players, or conversationalists, as well as by the less sociable drinkers.

The Awdrys' Jolly Party

FRANCIS KILVERT

Francis Kilvert was buried in Bredwardine, near Here-ford. He died aged thirty-eight in 1879. The inscription on his tombstone, 'He being dead yet speaketh', could not be more appropriate for a man whose diaries, when they were

· A Wiltshire Christmas ·

discovered and first published in 1938–40, opened a
window like no other on Victorian life and clerical
manners. Many of the diary entries describe events around
Chippenham, such as this account of a party held near
Lacock in early January 1873.

At 8 o'clock Fanny, Dora and I went to a jolly party at Sir John
Awdry's at Notton House. Almost everybody in the neighbourhood was there. There had been a children's party with a
Christmas Tree at 5 o'clock, but when we drove up the harp
and the fiddles were going. 'Bang went the drum, the ball
opened immediately, and I knew not which dancer most to
admire,' but I think it was – Francie Rooke. Dear little Francie
Rooke. The dining room was turned into the ball room,
beautifully lighted overhead, and the smooth polished oaken
floor went magnificently, just like glass, but not a bit too
slippery, though Eliza Stiles came down with a crash full on
her back in Sir Roger de Coverley, and there was a roar of
laughter which, combined with Eliza's fall, shook the room.

I danced a Lancers with Harriet Awdry of Draycot Rectory,
a quadrille with Sissy Awdry of Seagry Vicarage, a Lancers
with Louise Awdry of Draycot Rectory, a Lancers with Mary
Rooke of the Ivy, and Sir Roger with dear little Francie Rooke
of the Ivy. How bright and pretty she looked, so merry, happy
and full of fun. It was a grand Sir Roger. I never danced such a
one. The room was quite full, two sets and such long lines, but
the crush was all the more fun. 'Here,' said Francie Rooke to
me quietly, with a wild, merry sparkle in her eye, and her face
brilliant with excitement, 'let us go into the other set.' There
was more fun going on there, Eliza Stiles had just fallen
prostrate. There were screams of laughter and the dance was
growing quite wild. There was a struggle for the corners and
everyone wanted to be at the top. In a few minutes all order
was lost, and everyone was dancing wildly and promiscuously

Notton House, Lacock, where Kilvert danced in 1873. The house, seen here after snow in 1991, is now a Special school

with whoever came to hand. The dance grew wilder and wilder. 'The pipers loud and louder blew, the dancers quick and quicker flew.' Madder and madder screamed the flying fiddle bows. Sir Roger became a wild romp till the fiddles suddenly stopped dead and there was a scream of laughter. Oh, it was such fun and Francie Rooke was brilliant. When shall I have another such partner as Francie Rooke?

An excellent supper and we got home about one o'clock, on a fine moonlit night.

Carol Singing at Berwick St James

MRS D. COOK

Edith Olivier had a soft spot for old country ways, and part of her pioneer work for the Women's Institute movement in Wiltshire included compiling little books of traditional recipes and folklore, from contributions sent in by institute members. Here, from Mrs Cook of Berwick St James (between Wilton and Shrewton), are her memories of traditional carol singing, as recalled in 1930.

From far back beyond living memory, the men of Berwick have gone out carol-singing in the earliest hours of Christmas morning. The carols are not written, but handed down from generation to generation. There are recitative passages, too; and they end with:

> We wish you a merry Christmas,
> We *wish* you a merry Christmas,
> We wish you a merry *Christmas*
> And a *Happy* New Year!

It is a thrilling thing to be awakened in the dark or the moonlight of a Christmas morning, at about two o'clock, perhaps, by the powerful men's voices.

When we came here first we did not understand, and crept shivering out of bed to hurl down money and thanks (not perhaps of the heartiest). But it was explained to us afterwards that nothing is expected at that hour, but that the listeners shall stay snug in bed and realise that it is Christmas morning.

The carol singers come again in the evening of Christmas Day, and then is the time for thanks and shillings.

The words of the carols are more or less secret. One may write them down as one hears them, I suppose, but that, somehow, is not easy. Mr Kitley, of this village, who is 78 and who sang the carols for most of his lifetime, tried to get me a written record of them. 'I asked Tom Blanchard, and he wouldn't say as what he would and he wouldn't say as what he wouldn't.' Mr Blanchard seems to have special rights in the carols, because 70 years ago or more his great uncle, Isachar Blanchard, was leader both of the carol-singing and of the Berwick Band.

Isachar was 'a noted man with the violin'. He used to take his violin and accompany the carols with it. (I should like to note, in passing, that about 100 years ago the church music in Berwick used to be two violins and a bass viol.)

This year the words of the carols were written down for the use of some lads going out for the first time. But these were told to let no-one else see them.

Years ago, the singers used to practice on Christmas Eve in a house – now pulled down – that stood somewhere opposite the present Reading Room. At midnight they started out. In those days they did not go to Winterbourne Stoke. During the last dozen years or so the old customs have begun to break up. Nowadays the singers go to Winterbourne Stoke on Christmas Eve and have already sung there before they begin their singing in Berwick on Christmas morning.

Wiltshire Carols

The secrecy surrounding traditional carols, like that of the mummers plays, meant that the words seldom survive. When Alfred Williams in 1927 contributed an article on 'The Folk Carol in Wiltshire' to the Wiltshire Gazette *he could only give the words of two complete carols, and one of those came from Poulton, a Wiltshire village transferred to Gloucestershire in 1844. But as he said that it had been sung by the same family for 150 years I feel justified in including it here, along with his other example, from Castle Eaton near Cricklade. In 1890 the vicar of Harnham, Geoffrey Hill, published a collection of Wiltshire folk songs and carols, in which he included two short carols which he had heard sung at Britford near Salisbury. And in 1942 an early nineteenth-century carol, possibly from Clyffe Pypard near Wootton Bassett, was published alongside other miscellaneous folklore.*

From Poulton

> God sent for us the Sunday,
>   All with His holy hand,
> He made the sun fair, and the moon,
>   The water and dry land.
>
> There are six good days in the week,
>   All for a labouring man,
> The seventh day to serve the Lord,
>   The Father and the Son.

For the saving of your soul, dear man,
  Christ died upon the cross;
For the saving of your soul, dear man,
  Christ's precious blood was lost.

Three drops of our sweet Saviour's blood
  Were freely spilt for me;
We shall never do for our sweet Saviour
  As he has done for we.

My song is done, we must be gone,
  We stay no longer here;
So I wish you all a Merry, Merry Christmas,
  And a Happy New Year!

Carol singing on the steps of Salisbury Guildhall in 1951

· *A Wiltshire Christmas* ·

From Castle Eaton

Come, all you merry gentlemen, let nothing you dismay,
Remember Christ the Saviour was born on Christmas Day
To save poor souls from Satan's path long time been gone
  astray,
That brings tidings of comfort and joy.

When the shepherds heard those tidings it much rejoiced their
  minds,
They left their flocks a-feeding in tempest, storm and wind,
Straightway they came to Bethlehem and sang of God so kind,
That brings tidings of comfort and joy.

God bless the rulers of this house and all that dwell within,
God bless you and your children, I hope you heaven will win;
God bless you and your children that live both far and near!
And, good Lord, send us a joyful New Year!

From Britford

Rejoice, the promised Saviour's come,
  And shall the blind behold;
The deaf shall hear, and by the dumb
  His wondrous works be told.

Light from the sacred shore shall spread,
  O'er all the world shall beam,
In pastures fair shall all be led,
  And drink of comfort's stream.

The weary nations shall have rest,
  The rage of war shall cease,

· A Wiltshire Christmas ·

The earth with innocence be blest,
And plenty dwell with peace.

Also from Britford

Awake and join the cheerful choir,
　Upon this joyful morn.
And glad Hosanna loudly sing
　For joy a Saviour's born.

Let all the choirs on earth below
　Their voices loudly raise;
And sweetly join the cheerful band
　Of Angels in the skies.

The shining host in bright array,
　Descend from heaven to earth;
And all the gentle heart and voice
　Proclaim a Saviour's birth.

Perhaps from Clyffe Pypard

The first great joy our Mary had
It was the joy of one,
To see the blessed babe
Sucking at her breast bone,
Sucking at her breast bone good babe,
And blessed may she be,
With Father, Son and Holy Ghost
And all the blessed Three.

The next great joy our Mary had
It was the joy of two,
To see the blessed Jesus
Making the lame to go,
Making the lame to go, good man,
And blessed may he be,
With Father, Son and Holy Ghost
And all the blessed Three.

The next great joy our Mary had
It was the joy of Three,
To see the blessed Jesus
Making the blind to see,
Making the blind to see, good man,
Etc., etc.

The next, etc., the joy of four [*forgotten*].

The next great joy our Mary had
It was the joy of five,
To see the blessed Jesus
Making the dead alive,
Making the dead alive, good man,
Etc., etc.

The 6th, 7th and 8th joys forgotten

The next great joy our Mary had
It was the joy of nine,
To see the blessed Jesus
Turn water into wine,
Turn water into wine, good man,
Etc., etc.

Christmas Carol for the Year 1780

MICHAEL BURROUGH

*Unlike traditional carols here is one specially written, and
not published before. Its author was the mayor of Salisbury
who, elsewhere in this selection, is to be found giving us
indigestion with his poetic description of a feast.*

The pure the holy spotless Lamb, on this auspicious day
From heaven's glorious mansions come, to take our sins away.

This was amazing tenderness, this was stupendous love
Shown to a wretched sinful race, by God that reigns above.

For this with joy the earth it rings, with men's loud song of
    praise
To God the mighty king of kings, and angels joyn the joys –

Yet oh, our praises are too weak, our tongues too feeble are
Such grace, such wondrous love to speak, such goodness to
    declare.

But oh, th' eternal gratitude, that we are bound to pay
Commands our praises shold be shew'd, commands our thanks
    this day.

Hosanah to the Father be, hosanah to the Son,
Hosanah to the holy three, the blessed three in one.

Glory honour praise and power to the new God for ever
Jesus Christ is our redeemer, Halalujah praise the Lord.

Christmas

GEORGE HERBERT

Not a carol, but a Christmas poem by the saintly rector of Bemerton, near Salisbury. Herbert died and was buried here in 1633, and the volume of devotional poetry for which he is famous, The Temple, *was published in the following year.*

I

All after pleasures as I rid one day,
    My horse and I, both tir'd, body and mind,
    With full cry of affections, quite astray;
I took up in the next inn I could find.

There when I came, whom found I but my dear,
    My dearest Lord, expecting till the grief
    Of pleasures brought me to him, ready there
To be all passengers' most sweet relief?

71

Oh Thou, whose glorious yet contracted light,
  Wrapt in night's mantle, stole into a manger;
  Since my dark soul and brutish is thy right,
To Man of all beasts be not thou a stranger:

Furnish and deck my soul, that thou mayst have
A better lodging, than a rack, or grave.

II

The shepherds sing; and shall I silent be?
  My God, no hymn for thee?
My soul's a shepherd too; a flock it feeds
  Of thoughts, and words, and deeds.

George Herbert's church and rectory at Bemerton on the
outskirts of Salisbury

The pasture is thy word: the streams, thy grace
  Enriching all the place.
Shepherd and flock shall sing, and all my powers
  Outsing the daylight hours.
Then we will chide the sun for letting night
  Take up his place and right:
We sing one common Lord; wherefore he should
  Himself the candle hold.
I will go searching, till I find a sun
  Shall stay, till we have done;
A willing shiner, that shall shine as gladly,
  As frost-nipt suns look sadly.
Then we will sing, and shine all our own day,
  And one another pay:
His beams shall cheer my breast, and both so twine,
Till ev'n his beams sing, and my music shine.

The Other Wise Man

CHARLES HAMILTON SORLEY

*In contrast to Herbert's steadfast Christianity here is a
very different poem on a Christmas theme. We might these
days describe it as a 'green' carol, a reverent celebration of*

*nature. Its author, Charles Hamilton Sorley, had scarcely
left Marlborough College when he was killed on the
Western Front in 1915, and so his poetic genius had no
time to reach maturity. Many of his best poems, which
were first published in 1916, were written as a schoolboy
at Marlborough, and inspired, like this one, by the downs
and woods around the town. It is dated 1 December
1913, which means that it was written at the end of
Sorley's last term at the college.*

*(SCENE: A valley with a wood on one side and a road running up to a
distant hill: as it might be, the valley to the east of West Woods, that
runs up to Oare Hill, only much larger. TIME: Autumn. Four wise
men are marching hillward along the road.)*

ONE WISE MAN
I wonder where the valley ends?
On, comrades, on.

ANOTHER WISE MAN
  The rain-red road,
Still shining sinuously, bends
Leagues upwards.

A THIRD WISE MAN
  To the hills, O friends,
To seek the star that once has glowed
Before us; turning not to right
Nor left, nor backward once looking.
Till we have clomb – and with the night
We see the King.

ALL THE WISE MEN
  The King! The King!

A frosty morning along the road described by Sorley. It runs
up beside West Woods from Clatford to Oare Hill, near
Marlborough

THE THIRD WISE MAN
Long is the road but –

A FOURTH WISE MAN
   Brother, see,
There, to the left, a very aisle
Composed of every sort of tree –

THE FIRST WISE MAN
Still onward –

THE FOURTH WISE MAN
  Oak and beech and birch,
Like a church, but homelier than church,
The black trunks for its walls of tile;
Its roof, old leaves; its floor, beech nuts;
The squirrels its congregation –

THE SECOND WISE MAN
   Tuts!
For still we journey –

THE FOURTH WISE MAN
   But the sun weaves
A water-web across the grass,
Binding their tops. You must not pass
The water cobweb.

THE THIRD WISE MAN
   Hush! I say.
Onward and upward till the day –

THE FOURTH WISE MAN
Brother, that tree has crimson leaves.

· A Wiltshire Christmas ·

You'll never see its like again.
Don't miss it. Look, it's bright with rain –

THE FIRST WISE MAN
O prating tongue. On, on.

THE FOURTH WISE MAN
   And there
A toad-stool, nay, a goblin stool.
No toad sat on a thing so fair.
Wait, while I pluck – and there's – and here's
A whole ring . . . what? . . . berries?

(The Fourth Wise Man drops behind, botanizing)

THE WISEST OF THE REMAINING THREE WISE MEN
   O fool!
Fool, fallen in this vale of tears.
His hand had touched the plough: his eyes
Looked back: no more with us, his peers,
He'll climb the hill and front the skies
And see the Star, the King, the Prize.
But we, the seekers, we who see
Beyond the mists of transiency –
Our feet down in the valley still
Are set, our eyes are on the hill.
Last night the star of God has shone,
And so we journey, up and on,
With courage clad, with swiftness shod,
All thoughts of earth behind us cast,
Until we see the lights of God,
– And what will be the crown at last?

· *A Wiltshire Christmas* ·

ALL THREE WISE MEN
On, on.

(They pass on: it is already evening when the Other Wise Man limps along the road, still botanizing.)

THE OTHER WISE MAN
   A vale of tears they said!
A valley made of woes and fears,
To be passed by with muffled head
Quickly. I have not seen the tears,
Unless they take the rain for tears,
And certainly the place is wet.
Rain-laden leaves are ever licking
Your cheeks and hands . . . I can't get on.
There's a toad-stool that wants picking.
There, just there, a little up,
What strange things to look upon
With pink hood and orange cup!
And there are acorns, yellow – green . . .
They said the King was at the end.
They must have been
Wrong. For here, here, I intend
To search for him, for surely here
Are all the wares of the old year,
And all the beauty and bright prize,
And all God's colours meetly showed,
Green for the grass, blue for the skies,
Red for the rain upon the road;
And anything you like for trees,
But chiefly yellow, brown and gold,
Because the year is growing old
And loves to paint her children these.
I tried to follow . . . but, what do you think?

· A Wiltshire Christmas ·

The mushrooms here are pink!
And there's old clover with black polls,
Black-headed clover, black as coals,
And toad-stools, sleek as ink!
And there are such heaps of little turns
Off the road, wet with old rain:
Each little vegetable lane
Of moss and old decaying ferns,
Beautiful in decay,
Snatching a beauty from whatever may
Be their lot, dark-red and luscious: till there pass'd
Over the many-coloured earth a grey
Film. It was evening coming down at last.
And all things hid their faces, covering up
Their peak or hood or bonnet or bright cup
In greyness, and the beauty faded fast,
With all the many-coloured coat of day.
Then I looked up, and lo! the sunset sky
Had taken the beauty from the autumn earth.
Such colour, O such colour, could not die.
The trees stood black against such revelry
Of lemon-gold and purple and crimson dye.
And even as the trees, so I
Stood still and worshipped, though by evening's birth
I should have capped the hills and seen the King.
The King? The King?
I must be miles away from my journey's end;
The others must be now nearing
The summit, glad. By now they wend
Their way far, far, ahead, no doubt.
I wonder if they've reached the end.
If they have, I have not heard them shout.

Old Elijah

ALFRED WILLIAMS

George Herbert compiled a collection of proverbs, and number 840 says, 'They talke of Christmas so long, that it comes'. Well now we have reached Christmas Eve. We join Alfred Williams as he describes a cottage at Inglesham, between Highworth and Lechlade. It was published in 1922.

The few remaining days before Christmas passed by quickly. For a week the children had gone round to the farms every night, singing and begging. They carried lanterns made of swedes hollowed out, with a piece of candle fitted inside, and held them by the stump, warding off the draught with their hands. Then came 'Gooding Day' or 'Begging Day' – which is always eagerly looked forward to by the village children – and finally, the day before Christmas itself and the date of the proposed meeting at old Elijah's house.

A little before four o'clock the sun set, dropping down behind Lushill, and soon afterwards the station lamps at Highworth were lit, showing afar off like the lights of a ship at sea. The interior of Gramp's cottage was warm and bright. A fire of logs blazed up the chimney-back and a large lamp stood in the centre of the table beneath a rather low ceiling. Numerous pictures and photographs hung on the walls around. Above them were set sprigs of holly and mistletoe, or little boughs of ivy. On each side of the chimney was a recess fitted with cupboards and shelves containing dishes and chinaware, mugs and tumblers, gleaming in the merry firelight. The small clock on the mantlepiece was twenty minutes ahead of time. This is not an uncommon thing to find in the cottages, for the villagers love to be deceived in the matter of moments, and to feel that the hour is not really as far advanced as is indicated by the hands of the instrument. Inside the door was a thin partition to protect the fireplace from draught. Behind this old Elijah always sat, and never thought of shifting his position out of consideration for any.

Each of the visitors to the cottage had brought Gramp a small present. Clothes he needed not, nor yet a new pair of boots, for he seldom wore anything but slippers, either indoors or out. Books and newspapers were useless to him, for he could not see to read, and he had a sufficient stock of knowledge crammed into his old head to last him for the rest of his days. This his children and grandchildren knew, and so did not trouble to buy him anything that would be of no use. Instead they brought him a few good things to eat – cakes and oranges, a piece of beef for Christmas dinner, several ounces of tobacco, and a little flask of whisky. With all these Gramp was greatly pleased, though it was easy to see that he most preferred the tobacco and the small flask of barley juice, which, after all, was quite natural for one of his years. His delight in the tobacco was unbounded. 'Ho! ho! ho! H'm! h'm! h'm!' chuckled he, taking up the packages and holding them in his mouth one after another, and tossing his head the while, before he stowed them away on the shelf beside his pipe and spills, and sat down in the arm-chair with a triumphant expression upon his countenance.

Gramp was the hero of the hour. This he knew, though he tried to be natural and to conceal his joy at having the company present. His daughter called him 'a regular owl' toff' and teased him about wanting a 'hair-cut'. The children laughed and chattered like magpies, but old Elijah smiled the smile of one who is master of the situation and sat quietly and comfortably in his chair, smoking, and awaiting a convenient time for beginning the entertainment. He was dressed in corduroy trousers, with woollen waistcoat and cardigan jacket, and he had on a new felt hat such as is worn in the fields at haymaking. His wooden pipe was laid aside for a new clay with a long stem. His long snow-white hair fell gracefully over his shoulders and gave dignity to his form; he was really a grand old man, whose worth could not be over-estimated.

When the table had been cleared of the tea-things there came a lull in the conversation. Then Mrs Lawrence, Gramp's daughter, gave the fire a vigorous rout, brought more coals and set on the kettle again. Suddenly, without warning, Gramp burst into song with a clear, ringing voice, and we knew the time for festivity had arrived. He only sang one verse of the ditty. This was concerning two farmers who took refuge in the church porch during a heavy thunder-shower.

Several suggestions were made as to songs. One asked to hear 'The Jolly Tinker', or 'Preaching for Bacon,' others preferred 'Lord Bateman,' 'On the Banks of Sweet Dundee,' 'Butter and Cheese and All,' 'The Carrion Crow and the Tailor,' or 'The Oyster Girl,' all of which Gramp knew. Finally the matter was left for himself to decide.

Then Gramp said: 'Zeein' as we got a goodish company I thenks we ought to hae healths fust an' drenk to one another.'

A jug of ale was accordingly brought and the tumblers were reached down from the shelf. A little weak whisky and water, with sugar, was made for old Elijah. Then the glasses were clinked, and the young people stood up to drink.

'Now, then! What is it to be?' inquired Gramp of the first. Then the granddaughter replied:

'Here's a health to the world, as round as a wheel,

Death is a thing we all shall feel;
If life were a thing that money could buy
The rich would live, and the poor would die.'

'Aa! Tha's a very good un. Go on wi' t'other,' said Elijah.
Here the grandson spoke:

'Here's success to the plough, the fleece, and the flail,
May the landlord ever flourish and the tenant never fail.'

'Aa! Tha's a owld un, that is. I've yerd my grandfather saay
'e many a time when I was a bwoy. Wha's the next un?'
   Elijah's son spoke next:
'Here's a health to that as'll do that good when the body and
soul is taken from it!'
   'H'm, h'm, h'm. Tha's a teert un. Don' know the meanin' o'
'e – No.'
   'Yes you do know, too. What is it as does a ooman good
when 'er baby's born? You knows as my mother allus used to
gie a cup o' hot beer to the ooman as soon as the child was born
when 'er went a nursin'.'
   'Ah! ah! ah! To be sure. I forgot that. Tha's as much as to
say: "Yer's a health to the cup o' beer as doos the ooman good
when 'er baby's barn." Go on wi't.'

'Here's to the man with a ragged coat,
And with no means to mend it,
And here's to the man with plenty of cash,
And who doesn't know how to spend it.'

'H'm! h'm! 'E dwun' live at our 'ouse, nat the last un,
awhever. 'Ev 'e all done? Spose 'tis my time now then?' said
grandfather, rising from the chair and taking up his glass from
the table, while all eyed him eagerly. Holding the glass on

high and inclining his head a little to one side, old Elijah delivered his toast:

'Here's to the inside of a loaf and the outside of a gaol,
A good beefsteak and a quart of good ale,'

cried he, and drank off the contents of the glass amid much laughter.

'But you got neether beefsteak nor yet ale, for you drunk whisky an' water,' cried Mrs Lawrence.

There was no holding Gramp after that. His old face wore an ineffable expression, and he shook with frequent laughter. First he sang 'Paddle your own Canoe, my Boys,' then ran into 'The Four and Nine,' and ended with 'Blow the Candle out.' Afterwards followed a short bit of patter, then came 'Parson Jingle-Jaw's Adventure' and the song of 'Sweet Peggy O,' newly remembered after sixty years.

Just then a galloping of horses, accompanied by a loud rumbling sound, was heard outside.

'There goes the mailman from Lechlade! 'E's late to-night,' cried the hostess, looking up at the clock on the mantelpiece.

'Aa, 'e got a smartish load. 'E'll 'ev a job to get up Hywuth 'ill to-night. But dur-saay a got double 'osses. What! be 'e off a'ready, then? Thought 'e was gwain to stop a bit,' continued Elijah, as one of the company prepared to leave.

'Another half an hour and it will be Christmas morning,' replied he.

'Well! good-bye to 'e, if 'e *must* go. Look out for the owl' black dog o' Engleshum,' said Gramp, and the visitor, after wishing every one 'Goodnight,' and 'A Merry Christmas,' opened the door and left the cottage.

The night was calm and clear. Above Coleshill Wood the yellow half-moon was rising, topsy-turvy; the stars glittered brightly overhead in the frosty sky. Down below the sound of

the Cole leaping through the hatches could faintly be heard, otherwise there was perfect silence. The street lights were out in the town on the hill, but the old church tower stood black against the sky and was visible several miles off. As I passed beneath the dark trees a black dog came running by, and I thought of Gramp's parting words at the cottage, in which he referred to the Inglesham Ghost, though that was probably one let loose from the neighbouring farmyard.

Old Elijah became so merry after my departure that he stayed up till after two o' clock, and it was feared that he would not go to bed at all. Even after he was put there he kept singing, and only fell asleep an hour before daybreak, to wake again with a song when the postman's rat-tat came at the door signifying the arrival of the Christmas letters and parcels.

Christmas Eve at Sutton Evias

A.G. STREET

Sutton Evias is a fictional village, but to give an idea of the general area in which it is envisaged, Sutton Mandeville and Teffont Evias are neighbouring villages in the Nadder valley between Wilton and Tisbury, and the author of the novel from which this passage is taken was a

· A Wiltshire Christmas ·

farmer on the outskirts of Wilton. A.G. Street was born in 1892 and died in 1966. For him writing was a relaxation from his farm at Ditchampton, and he achieved fame with Farmer's Glory, *which was published in 1932. He followed this with a string of beautifully crafted novels, essays and broadcast talks, largely about life in the south Wiltshire countryside. It is from one of his novels,* The Gentleman of the Party, *of 1936, that the following extract comes. It is set on Christmas Eve, 1872.*

Then, when the maids came in to clear the table, Mrs Martin and her elder daughter retired to talk over the afternoon's purchases, the three other children proceeded to decorate the house with holly, and Farmer Martin stretched himself to sleep in an armchair near the blazing log fire. But although he lay there almost immovable until supper-time, he was never quite asleep. In a vague way his mind rambled over his farm, into Salisbury, along the road home, over the country of an imagined perfect run on the coming Boxing-day; in respectful conversation with his landlord, the Right Honourable, the Earl of Ashton, M.F.H.; in wranglings with that august gentleman's agent, Mr Hayward; in cogitation on market prices; on the ever-increasing deterioration of the farm labourer; on whether young George, his heir, would ever learn a bit of sense; on how much longer it would be before his daughter Carrie had young Ned Grant safely hooked; on the fact that although he, by almost superhuman cleverness and strenuous toil, just managed to make both ends meet, times were bad, devilish bad for farming; and that he had never known them worse.

In addition, he had one other worry, which was always present in his mind, even when his eyes were closed and his thoughts had almost jumbled him into unconsciousness. This concerned his feet. When a six-foot man lay in a comfortable

The traditional Boxing Day meet of the Wylye Valley Hunt in
Warminster Market Place during the 1950s

chair and stretched his legs out towards the blaze, no one save
himself realized what a large proportion of the room he
occupied, or how important it was that his beautiful semi-
conscious state of mind should not receive a rude shock by
someone falling over his feet. Besides, he had corns. So
when the children came in to put up the holly, or one of
the many maids was sent to make up the fire or to fetch
something for her mistress, no matter how quietly or
carefully they went about their business, they would be
certain to be greeted by a bellow from the master's chair,
'Mind my feet.'

In the kitchen and back regions of the farmhouse there was
great activity. Mrs Martin was a housewife; and a farm
housewife then, in spite of the fact that servants were cheap

87

and plentiful, had to be busy from dawn until bedtime; and at Christmas time she had to be specially busy. So that evening Mrs Martin harried her underlings and her children like a peppery colonel. Can it be wondered that the youngest of her four maids, little Alice Sturmey, aged fifteen, who scrubbed seemingly endless acres of stone floors and passages daily for the munificent wage of four pounds per annum and her keep, sometimes wondered if life were worth living? Still young 'Erby Goodridge's fierce hugs and awkward kisses came her way often enough to provide an affirmative answer. Very certainly, in her eyes they were worth a lot more than four pounds per annum, even worth the risk of her mistress finding out about them. That, of course, would be the end of the world so far as Alice was concerned, but until it happened, those kisses would be very sweet, the sweetest thing she had ever tasted.

In the men's cottages, too, there was much Christmas activity amongst the women and children, but in very few cases was the master of the house to be found at home. Once his tea had been swallowed and he had had a rough clean up, the married farm labourer went out until bedtime, which in most cases, the Christmas spirit being responsible, meant turn-out time down at the local pub, 'The Bell and Shoulder'. But even if he were a teetotaller, a chapel preacher, or, as his more ungodly neighbours put it, 'a bible-banger', or too worldly for the latter and too pleasure-loving for the former, the married agricultural labourer went out nearly every evening. There was no room in his cottage sacrosanct to his somnolent sprawl, no comfortable chair in which to rest his tired limbs, and generally a horde of children and a tired, nagging wife for company.

But in due time rich and poor, old and young, male and female, godly and ungodly, clerical and lay, drunken and sober – all the inhabitants of Sutton Evias save one were safely

in bed, and the Christmas moon shone over a silent world. In the best bedroom in the Manor Farmhouse the two rounded mounds of Farmer Martin and his good wife snored sonorously in a huge feather bed. In another George Martin and his little brother were sound asleep. In another little Mary snuggled close to her still wakeful elder sister; for Carrie lay thinking whether on the morrow Ned Grant would send her a present, which would be of such a nature as to prove his intentions beyond question.

In an upstairs attic little Alice Sturmey tossed and turned on her straw pallet; for, although she was so tired, she just could not sleep. She thought of 'Erby Goodridge, and of the strange but delightful feelings his caresses awoke in her. She remembered her mother's words about this, her first place. 'It ain't the money, Alice, wot matters. 'Tis the vittles. Missus Martin be strict and a mite near, but thee't get good grub.' She felt her rounded thighs and little swelling breasts, and remembered her skinniness of a year ago. She thought again of 'Erby, she wriggled her toes at ecstasy at this thought, and then, as a cloud obscured the moon and her little room became dark, she drifted into a happy slumber.

Down in the village every window was darkened, and every inhabitant save one safely in bed. Georgie Simmons lay four in a bed with his brother and sisters. His mother lay alone, wondering resentfully why she should have lost her man at such an early age, and whether it was too much to hope that some other man would want to satisfy her feminine needs before it was too late. Every other woman of her age in the village had her man lying beside her in bed. Why must she be the one to sleep alone?

But one other married woman of her age in Sutton Evias lay alone in her bed, and she was not a widow. Pigsticker Sam's wife lay sound asleep, while her husband pursued his nocturnal and nefarious activities under the massive humped shoulder of

Wexbury. Presently his figure showed black in the moonlight against the silver slope of Hungry Hill, but only for a moment or two. Sam knew better than to show up on a night landscape for very long. Soon his shape vanished into a hedge, after which there was no sign of him, until his agile figure nipped across the white main road, some fifty yards west of the turning to Sutton.

A few minutes later he crept up his garden path and entered his cottage by the back door.

'That you, Sam?' came his wife's voice from upstairs. 'The candle's on the table.'

'Shut thee girt mouth, oot,' answered her spouse, as he quietly locked the door of the cottage. He wanted no candle to light up his doings. The moon, drat it, gave light and to spare. Silently he crept across the room, and removed some loose floorboards under the kitchen table. Into the cavity beneath he placed three pheasants. Then, he replaced the boards, and crept to his chair by the dying fire, over the back of which lay his white Sunday shirt. Off came his boots, his jacket, and every garment save his undervest and his socks. On went the Sunday shirt, and up the narrow staircase went a bare-legged Pigsticker Sam. He slipped into bed beside his wife, with a satisfied grunt, and was soon asleep – something attempted and something done having earned his night's repose.

Then, until the Christmas dawn, the moon shone serenely over a silent world, in which a slinking fox and a coughing sheep were the only signs of life.

The Christmas Day Sequence

The body of liturgical observances and rituals which evolved first at Old Sarum and then in the present Salisbury Cathedral was known as the Use of Sarum. In the later middle ages it became popular and influential, and was adopted by many other English dioceses, so that it became the standard Latin service book of the English medieval church. From the first complete English translation of the Sarum Missal, published in 1868, here are three pieces of verse, known as sequences, which were chanted or spoken as part of the special Christmas masses, at midnight, daybreak and morning.

Christmas Day, at Midnight

All hosts with one accord
Sing the Incarnate Lord,
With instrument and breath,
Discoursing tidings glad.
This is the hallowed day
On which new happiness
Rose full upon the world;
On this renowned night
Glory was thundered forth,
By angel voices sung;

· A Wiltshire Christmas ·

Wondrous unwonted lights,
At midnight hour,
Around the Shepherds shone,
Keeping their quiet flocks.
All unexpectedly
God's message they receive.
Who was before the world
Is of a Virgin born;
Glory to God on high
In heaven, and peace on earth.
So doth the heavenly host
Sing praises in the highest,
Let heaven at either pole
Shake with their ringing chant.
On this most holy day
Let glory loudly sung
Through all the earth resound;
Let all mankind proclaim
That God is born on earth.
The foe shall vex mankind
With cruel rule no more;
Peace is restored to earth.
Let all creation joy
In Him Who now is born.
He all upholds alone,
He all did form alone:
May He of His own grace
Loose us from all our sins.

Christmas Day, at Daybreak

Unto the King new born praises sing,
Whose Father by His Word did frame the worlds,
Whose Mother is a Virgin undefiled;

Begotten of the Father, God of God,
Born of His Mother without carnal stain:
Before all worlds begotten of the Father;
When the full time was come His Mother bare Him.
O wonderful, mysterious generation!
O most astonishing Nativity!
O glorious Child! Divinity incarnate!
So Prophets, moved by Thy Holy Spirit,
Spake of Thy coming Birth, Thou Son of God!
So at Thy dawning Angels sing Thee praises,
And to the earth glad tidings bring of peace.
The very elements themselves are glad,
And all the Saints exultingly rejoice,
Crying, All hail! Save us, we pray, O God,
In Persons Trine, one undivided Substance.

Christmas Day, at the Third Mass

This day celestial melody
Was heard by men on earth,
When the Virgin bare a Son
The hosts above sang praise.
What aileth thee, thou world below?
Why joy'st thou not with these?
In pastoral charge the shepherds watch;
Hark! angels' voices clear
Chant forth their strains of holy joy,
Of peace and glory full;
To Christ they render homage due,
To us of grace they sing:
Not unto all such gifts are given,
But to men of good will;
Not irrespectively bestowed,
But measured by dessert;

Affections must be weaned from sin,
So shall that peace on us be shed
Which to the good is promised.
Earthly to heavenly things are joined,
In this respect their praises join,
But by desert they are dissever'd.
Rejoice, O man, when thou dost ponder this;
Rejoice, O flesh, associate with the Word.

His rising by the stars is told
    With indicating light;
Lo! star-lit chiefs to Bethlehem
    Follow that planet bright.
The King of Heaven is cradled found
    Amid the beasts He made,
In a rude manger's narrow bed
    The Lord of all is laid.
Star of the Sea! Thy Blessed Son
    The holy Church adores;
That Thou our service wilt accept
    Devoutly she implores.
Let each redeemed thing the Redeemer's praises sing.

An Outing for Angels

ELSPETH HUXLEY

*Best known for her foreign travel writing and biographies,
Elspeth Huxley in 1974 turned her pen to describing the
village of Oaksey near Malmesbury in north Wiltshire,
where she has lived since the 1950s. Her book, written as
a diary of her life in the village during a single year,
April 1974 to March 1975, was published under the title*
Gallipot Eyes *in 1976. Here is her entry for Christmas
Day, 1974, which her grandchildren spent with her.*

Well, it's over, the annual guzzle, peeling all those bright
wrappings from presents, stringing up gay cards destined all
too soon for the dustbin. So much care, skill and effort has
gone into the production of those cards, and some are so
attractive (Old Masters and birds and beasts particularly) that
it goes to my heart to throw them away. Often I've kept a few
favourite ones, to be used perhaps as book-markers, but in the
end they clutter desk or drawer and must go. What a world of
waste we inhabit.

The cottage reverberates with stentorian commands. 'NO,
Jos, that frog is Alexander's,' 'Leave Hugh's rabbit ALONE.'
Jos has taken to letting off steam, almost literally, with a
piercing high-pitched yell like a demonic engine. When the

boiler and the cats join in and the radio's going, even the Red Arrows couldn't make themselves heard.

The painted wooden angels have come out of the loft for their annual outing. They see the light for about three days and then hibernate, and aestivate, for the rest of the year, like characters in some Greek myth about fertility. They must be forty years old, bought for a few dollars on Madison Avenue and gradually matured into a family tradition. All with trumpets, wings and halos. One has lost her halo over the years.

Rain all day, thinning to a drizzle and then surging back into a storm. An afternoon walk across sodden fields towards the Swill Brook, all deserted, no cattle in the fields, only rooks flying over, an occasional blackbird chattering in a bare hedge, a solitary heron flapping slowly. It might have been the heron who deposited in the middle of a field a grey bivalve, former home of a Swan mussel.

Back to tea and Christmas cake, a faithfully observed tradition but after Christmas Day the cake hangs around and never gets finished; none of us is a tea-eater. 'NO, Jos, do NOT throw your fire-engine at your brother,' 'Yes, thank you for telling me that Hugh's been sick on the floor.'

After quiet reigns upstairs, a goose for our own dinner. I singed it, as advised by its breeder, out of doors, over a pan of methylated spirit, an alarming procedure amid leaping flames fanned by a strong wind. Eyebrows got more effectively singed than the goose.

Christmas without Daddy

SYBIL ECCLES

David and Sybil Eccles (Lord and Lady Eccles) made their home a farmhouse at Upper Chute near Ludgershall before the last war, but from 1939 until 1943 David was frequently abroad on diplomatic and government business. He pursued a distinguished political career, being elected to represent Chippenham in Parliament in 1943. He had two spells as Minister of Education, and was created Viscount Eccles in 1964. Sybil died in 1977. Their wartime correspondence was published in 1983, and here is Sybil's letter to her husband written on Boxing Day, 1940.

My dearest love – Christmas is nearly over. All about England tomorrow morning countless mothers will be waking with a sigh of relief – and many too, with tears that the stockings are emptied and they were not there to hear their children's cries.

We had a day of scrambles, as usual. Simon chose to collect a temperature of 102° on the Eve so he was in bed. I tried to console him for this – but he thought that *I* was worrying! and turned the tables on me with, 'Oh, don't worry, Mom – it's really quite all right – I don't mind a bit – I really quite like being in bed.'

St Mary's Church, Chute Forest, which is now redundant.
Built in 1875, it was designed by the noted Victorian
architect, J.L. Pearson

· A Wiltshire Christmas ·

We got over the stockings nicely in a grey, green mild December morning – then breakfast and presents. No tree – unless you count a tiny one for Simon's bedroom. Eleven o'clock was with us before the last parcel had been admired. Polly fell so violently in love with the doll we gave her (Annabella Eccles) that it was the hardest job to get her to look at anything else.

Away to St Mary's – which proved to be colder than it's ever been before and a round dozen of us shivered through the dreariest service that imagination could conceive. The dear Vicar lost himself in the middle and there were several agonising moments of atrocious stumbling!

Out we tottered, rubbing our blue hands and stamping our dying feet, and there was a conspicuous lack of Christmas uplift.

3 p.m. – and his Majesty – rather tired – rather lifeless – rather flat – but touching and probably went slap home to the heart of the Great Proletariat.

Then out into the black-out for Christmas evening. Anyway the boys enjoyed it, especially a game of shove-halfpenny played in two teams with half a crown for a prize.

John's team won in spite of *me* and the Captain pocketed the cash and, magnanimous in the hour of victory, remarked to his mother, to the huge amusement of the company, 'You weren't too bad, Mum, after all. You got one or two. I was glad to have you, you were quite useful on the whole,' and was quite disconcerted by the roars of laughter.

Midnight and in bed. 'Goodnight, Mum – it *was* a super party. A super super party. I wish Daddy had been there.' (Don't break it to him that Daddy would have hated it!)

All my love, dearest darling – Sybil

The Evacuees' Party

ENA BERRETT

The following extracts come from a diary kept by a young schoolteacher, Ena Berrett, at Hilperton near Trowbridge during 1940–1. I was delighted to discover that Miss Berrett still lives at Hilperton, in a bungalow now, and in her eighties, after a working life spent at the village school. These entries, which cover the whole Christmas period, refer to the same year as Sybil Eccles' letter, 1940.

Thursday 19 December **Mr Pearson** has been trying to get some sweets and oranges for the children but the shops had none. However he managed to get 10 lbs from Rose and Pavey's who make sweets in the town [Trowbridge]. We counted them out and put an equal number in each bag.

Friday 20 December Today we broke up for a fortnight. The children went home very pleased with their sweets and calendars they had made. It is a cold cloudy night. The siren sounded at 5.45 p.m. and the all clear did not go until 10.35 p.m. There were no search lights and we did not hear many planes, but we heard two bombs fall – one was rather loud.

Saturday 21 December The bomb we heard last night fell on Mr

Harding's farm at Beanacre. They say the windows in the farm house are broken. I went to Trowbridge on the bus to help my friend in her shop [Brown's in Roundstone Street]. Fruit is very scarce. Customers could only have two oranges and two onions each. It was a fine evening so I walked home – the sky was full of search lights – they searched the sky for the planes I could hear throbbing overhead.

Sunday 22 December A bitterly cold day – very few in church. The wireless went off the air after the 9 p.m. news.

Monday 23 December This morning Mr Evans the L.C.C. teacher came to see me about a party for the evacuee children. The director of education for the L.C.C. is in Devizes during the holidays to see that the evacuee children in the area are being well entertained. I went to Trowbridge again to help my friend. Chicken are 2/3d per lb this year. There was an alert from 6.30 p.m. until 1 a.m.

Tuesday 24 December Spent another busy day in the shop – each customer was allowed two oranges.

Wednesday 25 December No planes over today – seems good to be quiet. We invited our evacuees to spend the day with us and in spite of all the troubles we had a happy time together. We are growing very fond of them.

Thursday 26 December The weather is good. Pat the evacuee girl has a very bad cough. I went to town and managed to buy a lemon and some cough mixture for her. Mr Evans has asked Mrs Doris Matthews to organise a tea party for the evacuee children and she wants me to help her. We intend to include our own children.

Miss Berrett's snapshot of Pat, taken when she was an evacuee
in Hilperton during the last world war

· A Wiltshire Christmas ·

Friday 27 December I went to the Church Room to count the china.

Saturday 28 December A very quiet day. Many shops are still closed for the Christmas holiday.

Sunday 29 December I approached Major Mackay after church and told him about the party we were arranging for the children and he gave me £1 towards expenses. On the wireless last night we heard that a South-West town had been raided for the 240th time. We are wondering which town it is.

Monday 30 December Mr Pearson and Mr Evans called to discuss the party. We have decided to invite all the senior school children and high school children together with our junior school and evacuees making a total of 170. People are being very generous and have given up part of their margarine ration. I now have about 6 lbs.

Tuesday 31 December I spent most of the day collecting for the party. Mr Evans took me in his car.

Wednesday 1 January The weather has been against raids for a couple of nights. This afternoon Mrs Hibbert and I went to the Chapel to help wash the china ready for the party. It was cold and we were glad to get home. Several planes have gone over this evening.

Thursday 2 January 6.30 p.m. many planes about. 7.30 p.m. Trowbridge sirens sounded. Planes flying very low. We had snow last night and several snow storms during the day. I tried to buy some white knitting wool but there was none to be had. We went to the Chapel this evening and put up the tables and laid them ready for the party tomorrow.

Friday 3 January A busy day. We spent the morning cutting up, for the 170 children. We had enough food and some to spare, and the children had a happy time. The sirens went at 6.30 p.m. – we did not hear them which is not surprising. As we were going home we saw a bright glow in the sky in the eastern direction. Search lights were busy.

Saturday 4 January Bristol had a heavy raid last night. When Mr Harding came with the milk this morning he told us that at 6 a.m. the sky over Bristol was all aglow. Our all clear sounded at 6.20 a.m. British planes have been very busy all day flying in formation in all directions. Formations of bombers were accompanied by Spitfires. We spent a busy morning clearing up after the party – sorting china and stacking it away. It is bitterly cold and there is still snow around.

A Day of Black Disaster

GEORGE ATWOOD

George Atwood was rector of Bishopstrow near Warminster from 1883 until his death in 1921, and his unpublished diaries, in a sometimes illegible scrawl, are

preserved in the Wiltshire Record Office. These extracts, from Christmas 1913, sum up nicely his character and attitudes.

Monday 22 December Fine, dull. This morning went into Warminster. Saw Wakeman about the girl Legge – she's not feeble minded but *wicked*. Also saw Ponting about the water at Norton in case the diphtheria case can be traced to it. Then on to the garage and the club. Gave my contribution to the steward and stewardess's Xmas box, and took old Cole Hamilton in and made him do the same. Then home to lunch and at 2 o'clock Herbert A'Court took me to Trowbridge – Dick being in London trying on his new dress clothes!!! Call at the Assoc'n Office no good the Agent in Warminster. Home to

The minster church (St Denys), Warminster under snow during the hard winter of 1962–3

105

tea at Eastleigh. Also saw Gratney and Harry Laverton. Home to dinner. I am glad to say my remedy of last night quite effective – finest medicine there is!

Tuesday 23 December Rain all day without ceasing. In the morning went into Warminster. Got some Xmas presents. Went to Wakeman's office about that girl – also up to the Union. Saw Bradbury and the master about Xmas matters. Lunched with the Burtons then muddled about at home until tea time. I should have gone up to the Reformatory but it was really too wet for anything. The Ladies decorated the Church today as it was more convenient than doing it on Wednesday; the real reason being that the hounds meet at Greenhill today and most of them want to be there. I posted numerous cards of Xmas wishes and suchlike rubbish. Went to a choir practice in the evening.

Wednesday 24 December Fine and frosty. Started at quarter to ten to shoot with Lord B [Bath]. Party was Gratney, Mont-gomerie, John Thynne, Crutwell, Col. Ruggles-Brice and self. We had quite a good day, about 400 – and several woodcock, six I think. Came home about five. Picked up some things in Warminster. Went in and saw Herbert A'Court. Lord B. gave me two woodcock, one of which I gave to old Wakeman, as I know no man who will enjoy it more. Then dinner and bed. I am still a bit wobbly about the tum-tum, but hope it will wear off.

Thursday 25 December Fine frosty morning, rain p.m. Service at 8 a.m. 37 communicants; 11 a.m. 26 communicants. Lunched with the Southeys at Eastleigh, and directly after I started off. Went to the Workhouse it poured with rain. Saw or went through all the sick wards, and wished the poor old folk the good wishes of the season. Very pleased with all I saw,

Christmas in a children's ward at Salisbury Infirmary, 1924

then on to the Reformatory still pouring with rain. And saw all the boys at tea. Said a few words to them then back just in time to dress for dinner at the Bruces. A family dinner party. Bertie and Hazel there with the others I am glad to say.

Friday 26 December Drizzle and cold. Went at 10.30 to Longbridge Deverill to shoot snipe. Met the guns at Crockerton. Col. Ruggles-Brice, Lord Bath, Lord Weymouth, W. Montgomerie, self. We had an excellent drive out of the big marsh, but no other luck all day. Shot 15 snipe (about) and a few pheasants in the withy bed. But although not a great bag had a pleasant day. Driver Peter. Called on Wakeman on my way back and told him I could not come to the meetings on Saturday. I did this with regret but I have given up so much shooting for business this year I felt justified.

· A Wiltshire Christmas ·

The ice has almost completely closed over the lake in this view of Shearwater, on the Longleat estate, which was taken after snow in 1991

Saturday 27 December Fine frosty. Shot duck at Shearwater. We distributed ourselves round the lake, Lord B., Gratney and self – the other three guns on the Longleat Ponds. Lionel, Harry and Mabel came out and sat with me during first drive. We got all told between 50 and 60 duck and teal. Dined at the Bruces.

Sunday 28 December Dull inclined to snow. Services at 11 o'clock and 6. Good congregations considering the day. Bertie and Hazel came to lunch and stayed to tea. Cole Hamilton came to supper.

Monday 29 December Snow on ground, cold north wind. My birthday and a most uncomfortable day. No breakfast to speak

of. All cold and miserable. My sandwiches all wrong and packed in a portmanteau-like parcel. Could not take them to the Board so had to work on an empty stomach until I got home from the Board at 3.30. I then got a cup of luke-warm Bovril, and practically had nothing to eat until tea at 4.30. If I lived as well as the cats I should be a happy man – who at least have their food well and carefully cooked and served hot. I should have thought a husband was of as much importance as a cat, but apparently not. Heard from Toby. (The two people who remembered my birthday were Maria, dear little girl, and Mrs Cochrane)

Tuesday 30th December Fine frosty. A day of black disaster. I started in the morning by a mistake. I thought Gratney was shooting at Black Dog but he was not so I had to telephone in a hurry to the Motor Works for a car. They sent over one driver viz John Bush, a most respectable man and good driver. The roads were awful, so slippery. And we had to drive with great caution. I was late but this did not matter. After shooting was over at 4 o'clock no car had arrived to take me back, so at Lord Bath's suggestion I started to walk up the hill, he promising to wait for me, squeeze me in somehow and take me on if no car turned up. Almost directly he came running up saying an accident had happened – that a car was all across the road upside down and the driver under it. We rushed up and I found poor Bush quite dead – his skull fractured, his shoulder broken and other injuries – he had skidded and turned over. Thank God death was instantaneous.

Wednesday 31st December Fine frosty. I did not shoot this day. I felt after poor Bush's death it would not be respectful to his memory. So I went in to the garage and saw if there was anything I could do to help things in any way – but there was not. I then went up to the Union, and was kept so long I could

not go to lunch with the Cochranes as I intended. In the evening I dined at Greenhill to meet Sir Oliver Lodge. He is a great scientist and a charming man but if he finds coal here I will never forgive him – fancy turning little peaceful Bishopstrow into a great howling mining village. It makes me sick to so much as think of such a thing. So ends a *most disastrous year, 1913. FINIS.*

Christmas Ale and a Sad Nativity

Reading a parish register, as anyone who has tried to trace his ancestors will tell you, can be about as exciting as reading a telephone directory. Most are little more than lists of names and dates, and often centuries of neglectful storage, or the parson's arthritic handwriting, make them trying and tedious documents to read. But every now and then someone has seen fit to record a notable event or a matter which seemed at the time to be of great parochial importance, and then a touch of humanity shows through. Here are extracts from two seventeenth-century registers, which inform us of a celebration and a tragedy which occurred at Christmases long ago. First, a series of memoranda scrawled in the earliest parish register for Everleigh, near Upavon.

· A Wiltshire Christmas ·

When I came first to this parish, being now about eleaven or twelve yeares past, it was said there had been a custome longe before of making the neighbourhood eate (only bread and cheese) and drinke at the parsonage house on Christmas day after eveninge prayer, which custome out of neighbourlie kindness, or out of weaknesse (for I misliked it) I continued accordingelie till the gunpowder treason 1605. After which tyme wee agreed both I and the parishioners (except one or two) that that drinkeinge should be on the fifth of November, in remembrance of the deliverance, which continued some few yeares, but after they desyred to have it on their old day, and so had it. This present 9th of September 1610. – John Banstone.

I ever required and claymed of my neighbours a custome from them in lieu of this custome, as both reason and example of other parishes persuaded mee; but they either know it not, or conceale it. – JB.

The survival of this Christmas Ale, as it must have been, continued to upset Mr Banstone's successors:

. . . I continued (invita Minerva '*against my better judgement*') to avoyd the clamours of the under sort of the parish, who flock to it as to a Christmas pastime; I could never learne how this heathenish custome had its first birth originall. Sure I am it is of evil report, and no man can imagine into what rudeness in tract of time it may degenerate. It were to be wisht, that it now layd in the dust, and utterly forgotten. Thomas Ernle rector, Anno Dom. 1667, December 25.

But clerical disapproval had no effect:

Memorandum. When I came to this living I found two very bad customs for which no reason can be assigned. One is the

entertainment of bread and cheese and ale on Christmas Day; but on the alteration of the style *{the change to the calendar made in 1752}* I removed it to the 5th of Jany . . . This 16th May 1755, A. Le Moine.

> *And that is the last we hear of an ancient custom. The second group of extracts is taken from one of the registers of Fisherton Delamere near Wylye. The incumbent here was a certain Thomas Crockford, and it was his habit to record (in Latin so that his parishioners would not be able to read them) brief biographical details of everyone who occurs in his registers. Here a family's Christmas tragedy is reported with a simplicity which makes it all the more poignant:*

Elizabeth Pierson or Vargeis the elder, spinster daughter of John Pierson or Vargeis, farmer of Bapton, and his wife Catherine; she suffered from epilepsy and finally died on 16th December [1617], and was buried on the 17th.

George Vargeis, the illegitimate son of Elizabeth Vargeis the younger, daughter of John Vargeis or Pierson, farmer of Bapton, was born on the 17th and baptized on the 19th of December 1617.

Elizabeth Pierson or Vargeis the younger, another daughter of John Pierson or Vargeis, farmer of Bapton, and his wife Catherine. She was a girl deceived by the attentions of a false and good-for-nothing boyfriend, by the name of Durham, who took her virginity after leading her on with the prospect of marriage. It is said that, worn out by the pain of childbirth, she languished repentantly for a little while, and then expired. She died and was buried on Christmas Day, 25th December [1617].

George Pierson or Vargeis, illegitimate son of the foresaid Elizabeth, a very small baby, died and was buried on 31st December.

And if we browse through the register we find the parents,
John and Catherine, a few pages later. He died in October
1619, and she in September 1621, both aged about sixty.
Their eldest son, George, died six weeks after his father,
in December 1619.

Drove Road, Swindon, in 1908

Tha Snow

EDWARD SLOW

Except in passing we have not yet considered the question of
the appropriate seasonal weather. Here is the mayor of
Wilton again to introduce us to a few white Christmases.

113

· *A Wiltshire Christmas* ·

Tha snow, tha snow, is vallen,
An my good deam, she be callen,
'Be quick, good man, hie out a tha starm,
An com to yer snug leetle cottage, za warm'.

Tha snow, tha snow, ael droo tha snow,
Away to his wirk tha poor man mist go;
Bit, ah, wen at nite a greets his snug cot,
An smills his hot zupper, his keers be vargot.

When tha snow lays deep and vrosts da bite,
An tha vields an downs be covered quite,
Tha leabourer sturdy, up in the vield barn,
Be-leabours ael day tha russet brown carn.

Tha vrost an tha snow tho cheerless they zeems,
Tha zweets that thay avs ther roughness redeems;
Var where will ee vine a cozier zite
Than a leabourer's cot on a cwould winter's nite.

Gastard Sunday Morning

Yesterday's snow, delivered horizontally with venom, was mostly gone by nightfall, but we woke this morning to the real thing. It was the stuff of robins and jingle bells, and it was falling as it is supposed to – vertically, slowly, and the size of cornflakes. What is more, the weather-god obligingly switched it off as soon as we had finished breakfast.

Sunday mornings are quiet where we live and you cannot, as in towns, gauge the muffled acoustic of overnight snow from your bed. It is the visual impact here, of accustomed fields rendered colourless, a monochrome landscape.

The morning walk is different today. Yesterday, in the savage wind, we ventured no further than the garden, and the first snowfall of a young dog's life was celebrated with frenzied circuits of high excitement. But today the experienced snow-dog strides out along the road, past a neighbour's step already swept (the snowing has barely stopped), past a field of dreary-grey sheep (each with a no-fun-for-us! stare), and across the field to Thingley.

The trailing edge of the snowcloud is in front of us now, and behind it blue sky and a hesitant sun are starting to paint the colours back on to the hillside beyond Lacock. The trees are already dripping.

At Thingley we reach a lane unviolated by tyre tracks. As a student of roads, I often try to imagine ancient lanes such as

· A Wiltshire Christmas ·

Winter landscape with dog, near Thingley, Corsham

this before they were dressed with tarmac – rutted, grass-grown and of wavering width. Today it is easy. The snow has buried the twentieth century, and the lane greets us afresh as it would have done a medieval traveller on a winter's day six hundred years ago. We are the first of all creation to exercise this right of way today. The new snow sticks to my boots and falls off in lumps.

Ten minutes later we are playing snowballs across a field, when the Canada geese arrive. They are a noisy squadron, and we seem to lie under the flight-path of their morning constitutional from the lake in Corsham Park. I stop to count them. Fifty-nine, I think, but one of them is completely white. A snow-goose? Surely not.

We return home. Past a yesterday's snowman on a garden wall, past a cautious procession of motorists on the slushy main road, past a father with two young children dragging their new toboggan (its first outing to the playing field, their first real snow ever, perhaps). It is bright sunshine now. Already, I imagine, next year's Christmas card photographers are loading their equipment and setting off in their cars for Castle Combe.

The dog, dried-off, will go to sleep. And I shall switch the heater on in my study – but first, was it a snow-goose? Do you see snow-geese in Wiltshire? My book says that you don't, or rather, '*Anser caerulescens*, Vagrant (escape)' – only three since records began. But then, you don't see snow very often, these days.

Footprints at Longleat

ELIZABETH HAMILTON

During the Second World War Longleat was occupied by a girls' school, and one of the teachers who found herself in such magnificent surroundings was Elizabeth Hamilton. She subsequently wrote novels, biographies and religious works, but her first book was a description of the changing seasons at Longleat. Entitled The Year Returns, *it was*

· A Wiltshire Christmas ·

published in 1952, and here are some evocative wintry passages taken from it.

Snow on the roof: picking out the scallops on the cupolas; resting on the noses of the stone dogs; wrapping the shoulders of the statues and clinging in the folds of their draperies; coating the balustrade and parapets, smooth like sugar-icing. Snow on the oak-trees' nobbled branches and filling the scars and crevices upon the trunk. Snow brimming the beech-cups and tipping the pointed twigs; and bowing to earth the cedar's giant branches.

Snow hanging in soft drifts on tangled reed-beds, and streaking the black ice upon the lake, like veins in marble.

Snow in sunshine, scintillating with a thousand diamond lights, and patterned with the blue shadows of limes and cypresses, and the racing shadows of duck on the wing. Snow splashed with the crimson of the setting sun. Snow when the sun has set but the moon has not yet risen; a dead, flat whiteness: no light, no sparkle; and all about a lonely, muffling silence.

Quiet-eyed cattle shiver in their staring coats, and their breath is as smoke upon the freezing air. Hay, spread on the snow for fodder, glows like golden hair; and all about it gather hungry birds: rose-breasted chaffinches, greenfinches with flashing yellow on their wings, a creamy song thrush, and the larger, greyer, mistle-thrush; sooty male blackbirds and dusky females; bold tits and squabbling sparrows.

On the window-sill the snow is etched with the arrowhead marks of tiny claws, one level with another, in parallel lines that end abruptly where the bird has taken flight; or with a gash when a wing has cut the snow.

In the yard the drifts that shroud the rugged heaps of coal are patterned with the filigree tracks of mice, and a rat's lean, pointed claws. On garden paths a dog has left his zigzag

The view from Heaven's Gate across Longleat Park as the
morning's snowfall begins to melt

prints; lopsided and clumsy in contrast with the cat's neat,
round steps, that are placed fastidiously in a straight line.

The park's vast whiteness shows the cloven tracks of racing
deer; a solitary hare's direct and dashing course; and, every-
where, the restless, swerving prints of rabbits. Up on the
slopes under the beeches, a badger's ponderous 'bars' have sunk
into the snow; and a pheasant has left the clear-cut marks of
three smooth toes and the sweep of his drooping tail.

Alongside the frozen lake a fox's steps lead sometimes to
higher ground (was it from here he looked about him, snuffing
the air?), and then down again to the ice; the tidy tracks of
pear-shaped pads; three toes or maybe four, and the trace of
nails; and, where he has made a sudden turn, the imprint of a
tail-tip. By the lake, too, you can see the marks of a moorhen's

slender toes set far apart, in lines, criss-crossing one another, and the wider, flatter toe-prints of coots and grebes; and largest of all a swan's 'paddles', sunk deep and soft into the snow.

Rose-petal clouds float in a turquoise sky; and swans, rose-tinted, like creatures of a dream, sail on an ink-black pool among the green, encircling ice.

The oak is a crystal tree: every twig encased in shimmering ice. Ice hangs in tassels from the fountain-bowl; and drapes the children carved in stone beneath it. Yew hedges, topped with white, become giant slabs of Christmas cake.

Skating

RICHARD JEFFERIES

To compile a Wiltshire anthology without including something by Richard Jefferies would be unthinkable. Born in 1848 at Coate, which used to be a great deal further away from Swindon than it is now, this son of a small farmer worked first as a journalist, and then made a precarious living writing essays, novels and books about natural history and the countryside. Long championed by enthusiasts in north Wiltshire, his work has now under-gone a revival; most of his prolific output has reappeared in print, and his descriptions of Victorian country life are once again being enjoyed and admired by a wide reader-

· A Wiltshire Christmas ·

ship. Here is an essay which was not published during his lifetime (he died at the age of thirty-nine in 1887), but was collected by his biographer, the poet Edward Thomas, and included in The Hills and the Vale, *in 1909.*

The rime of the early morning on the rail nearest the bank is easily brushed off by sliding the walking-stick along it, and then forms a convenient seat while the skates are fastened. An old hand selects his gimlet with the greatest care, for if too large the screw speedily works loose, if too small the thread, as it is frantically forced in or out by main strength, cuts and tears the leather. A bad gimlet has spoilt many a day's skating. Nor should the straps be drawn too tight at first, for if hauled up to the last hole at starting the blood cannot circulate, and the muscles of the foot become cramped. What miseries have not ladies heroically endured in this way at the hands of incompetent assistants! In half an hour's time the straps will have worked to the boot, and will bear pulling another hole or even more without pain. On skates thus fastened anything may be accomplished.

Always put your own skates on, and put them on deliberately; for if you really mean skating in earnest, limbs, and even life, may depend on their running true, and not failing at a critical moment. The slope of the bank must be descended sideways – avoid the stones concealed by snow, for they will destroy the edge of the skate. When within a foot or so, leap on, and the impetus will carry you some yards out upon the lake, clear of the shadow of the bank and the willows above, out to where the ice gleams under the sunshine. A glance round shows that it is a solitude; the marks of skates that went past yesterday are visible, but no one has yet arrived: it is the time for an exploring expedition. Following the shore, note how every stone or stick that has been thrown on by thoughtless persons has sunk into and become firmly fixed in

the ice. The slight heat of midday has radiated from the surface
of the stone, causing the ice to melt around it, when it has
sunk a little, and at night been frozen hard in that position,
forming an immovable obstacle, extremely awkward to come
into contact with. A few minutes and the marks of skates
become less frequent, and in a short time almost cease, for the
gregarious nature of man exhibits itself even on ice. One spot
is crowded with people, and beyond that extends a broad
expanse scarcely visited. Here a sand-bank rises almost to the
surface, and the yellow sand beneath causes the ice to assume a
lighter tint; beyond it, over the deep water, it is dark.

Then a fir-copse bordering the shore shuts out the faintest
breath of the north wind, and the surface in the bay thus
sheltered is sleek to a degree. This is the place for figure-
skating; the ice is perfect, and the wind cannot interfere with
the balance. Here you may turn and revolve and twist and go
through those endless evolutions and endless repetitions of
curves which exercise so singular a fascination. Look at a
common figure of 8 that a man has cut out! How many
hundreds of times has he gone round and round those two
narrow crossing loops or circles! No variation, no change; the
art of it is to keep almost to the same groove, and not to make
the figure broad and splay. Yet by the wearing away of the ice
it is evident that a length of time has been spent thus for ever
wheeling round. And when the skater visits the ice again, back
he will come and resume the wheeling at intervals. On past a
low waterfall where a brook runs in – the water has frozen
right up to the cascade. A long stretch of marshy shore
succeeds – now frozen hard enough, at other times not to be
passed without sinking over the ankles in mud. The ice is
rough with the aquatic weeds frozen in it, so that it is
necessary to leave the shore some thirty yards. The lake
widens, and yonder in the centre – scarcely within range of a
deer-rifle – stand four or five disconsolate wild-duck watching

every motion. They are quite unapproachable, but sometimes an unfortunate dabchick that has been discovered in a tuft of grass is hunted and struck down by sticks. A rabbit on ice can also be easily overtaken by a skater. If one should venture out from the furze there, and make for the copse opposite, put on the pace, and you will be speedily alongside. As he doubles quickly, however, it is not so easy to catch him when overtaken: still, it can be done. Rabbits previously netted are occasionally turned out on purpose for a course, and afford considerable sport, with a very fair chance – if dogs be eschewed – of gaining their liberty. But they must have 'law', and the presence of a crowd spoils all; the poor animal is simply surrounded, and knows not where to run. Tracks of wild rabbits crossing the ice are frequent. Now, having gained the farthest extremity of the lake, pause a minute and take breath for a burst down the centre. The regular sound of the axe comes from the wood hard by, and every now and then the crash as some tall ash-pole falls to the ground, no more to bear the wood-pigeon's nest in spring, no more to impede the startled pheasant in autumn as he rises like a rocket till clear of the boughs.

Now for it: the wind, hardly felt before under shelter of the banks and trees, strikes the chest like the blow of a strong man as you rush against it. The chest responds with a long-drawn heave, the pliable ribs bend outwards, and the cavity within enlarges, filled with the elastic air. The stride grows longer and longer – the momentum increases – the shadow slips over the surface; the fierce joy of reckless speed seizes on the mind. In the glow, and the speed, and the savage north wind, the old Norse spirit rises, and one feels a giant. Oh that such a sense of vigour – of the fulness of life – could but last!

By now others have found their way to the shore; a crowd has already assembled at that spot which a gregarious instinct has marked out for the ice-fair, and approaching it speed must

· A Wiltshire Christmas ·

A Snowball fight on the canal bridge by Quaker's Walk,
Devizes. The photograph probably dates from the 1880s and
must have been taken under rather difficult conditions

be slackened. Sounds of merry-laughter, and the 'knock,
knock' of the hockey-sticks arise. Ladies are gracefully gliding
hither and thither. Dancing-parties are formed, and thus
among friends the short winter's day passes too soon, and
sunset is at hand. But how beautiful that sunset! Under the
level beams of the sun the ice assumes a delicate rosy hue;
yonder the white snow-covered hills to the eastward are rosy
too. Above them the misty vapour thickening in the sky turns
to the dull red the shepherd knows to mean another frost and
another fine day. Westwards where the disc has just gone
down, the white ridges of the hills stand out for the moment
sharp against the sky, as if cut by the graver's tool. Then the

vapours thicken; then, too, behind them, and slowly, the night falls.

Come back again in a few hours' time. The laugh is still, the noise has fled, and the first sound of the skate on the black ice seems almost a desecration. Shadows stretch out and cover the once gleaming surface. But through the bare boughs of the great oak yonder the moon – almost full – looks athwart the lake, and will soon be high in the sky.

A True Relation

So far we have looked at snow and ice from the Christmas card point of view, picturesque and fun. But of course there is another side to it. Here is a chapbook published in 1685.

A TRUE RELATION of a great number of people frozen to death near Salisbury, and in several other parts of the West of England, on Tuesday, the twenty-third of December, 1684, besides horses and much other cattle.

The dismal truths contained in this paper will need no preamble to induce a belief thereof in the reader; they are no stories of what happened in former kings' reigns, or an account of things done in Prester John's dominions, easier to be believed than disproved. But a dreadful relation fit to be recorded in the chronicle for after ages, and a present

astonishing dispensation of God Almighty, which calls for the serious consideration of all Englishmen.

On Tuesday, the 23rd of December, 1684, the weather being cold and freezing, there likewise happened a terrible, and certainly the most dreadful storm hath in these nations been heard of in the memory of man. To give the particulars from every part of the kingdom, would take up many sheets; and what I yet have exactly, is from the western parts thereof.

The carriers from London, to Exeter, Taunton, Shaftesbury, Bath, and Wells, etc., going as usually out from London on Saturday, and particularly the 20th of December, 1684, and in pursuance of their respective journeys, being on Tuesday the 23rd with their horses and passengers, to pass the Downs on this side Salisbury: such of them as escaped, and returned to London, do relate the manner of the storm in those parts to be as followeth, viz. That the wind being all day north-east, and violently cold, about two in the afternoon it began to snow very fast, and held on till two or three a clock next morning, the wind continuing fierce, and blowing it in such heaps, that in some places the snow lay as high as a house top, in others the ground scarcely covered, which so altered the roads, especially upon the Downs and Plains, that (although some of them had weekly used the same roads for thirty or forty years together) none of the said carriers could that night either find the way to their inns, or any towns they might get shelter, but themselves, their passengers, and horses forced to wander about till many of them were frozen to death, who before the storm began, were hearty and healthful. Each of the said carriers labouring, and being lost several miles distant from the other.

Mr Mathews the carrier of Shaftesbury had his unfortunate lot within fifty-six miles of London, two miles on this side Stockbridge, who albeit he escaped with life, yet his hands are frozen up, that he hath lost the use of them, and two of his horses dyed with extremity of cold upon the Downs that very night.

Mr Morris the younger carrier to Exeter; also Mr Clark the elder, who carries to Shaftesbury, Evil [Yeovil], and other parts, with their horses and passengers were lost upon the Downs, six miles beyond Stockbridge; there in like manner wandring all night to an again, by continual action and labour were preserved alive.

Mr Collins the Taunton carrier, and Mr *** the carrier to Bath and Wells, with their gangs of horses and passengers travelled that day, about two miles distant from each other; were passing between Andover and Amesbury, and when first lost, judged they might want five or six miles of Amesbury.

The Wells carrier being foremost, had two of his company frozen to death, viz. his own son, a youth about thirteen or fourteen years of age, and a young man, a passenger aged about twenty years; which persons were not parted from the rest, or smoothered in the snow, but absolutely frozen to death, as they rode or walked along in company. This distressed carrier's bowels yearning as he saw his son grow stiff and faint, got him up, and carried him till he dyed in his arms, and after he was dead, carried him on horseback; until extremity of cold forced him to let him drop upon the Down and leave him.

Neither had Mr Collins who carries to Taunton and Tiverton less misfortune; a man and his wife, two hearty antient people, being of his passengers, and riding on single horses, altho' very healthful and well in the morning, and chearful in the afternoon, yet by the continued cold and stragling of the poor horses, or by their own growing feeble to manage them, lost sight of the gang, and wandred by themselves, till at length they lay down and dyed one at the feet of the other.

Mr Collins himself and servants, when within three miles of Amesbury, hapned upon a parish where they hired a guide for

ten shillings, who undertook to lead their bell horse, and conducted them a mile and a half of the three; when going faster than they could follow, Mr Collins beg'd of him for Gods sake to go no faster than they were able to come with the other horses.

But the guide, alledging his own life was in danger, kept on his pace, and got safe to the Bear Inn at Amesbury by nine o'clock at night; Mr Collins, his servants and horses wandering till six in the morning, and then discovering an old barn, broke into it for shelter till day light, one of his said servants is like to loose the use of his limbs, and Mr Collins with the rest, meerly (under God) by violent labour and busling saved their lives.

The servant of the Lady Fines of New-Tony, in the county of Wilts, having been that day at Salisbury market, in his return with a cart and two horses, lost himself upon the same Down, and having tyed his fore-horse-head to the cart, was found

Wroughton High Street, 1908

dead near them, by eight of the clock that evening, and being within half-a-mile of Amesbury: the servants of the Bear Inn, coming out to look for the carriers, found him in manner as aforesaid.

A shop-keeper living near Chauke [Broad Chalke], a place in those parts, also perished in coming from Salisbury market.

Six or seven country-people, in passing from Chard to Ilmester, though but three or four miles distance, were by the way frozen to death.

One Mr Knight of Evil [Yeovil], a market-town of Somerset, in a letter to a friend in this city, affirms, about thirty people from that town and parts adjacent, that went the same day to markets, or after other concerns, were not heard of, except some few found dead.

About Tiverton many in like manner perished as they went from markets. Between Plymouth and Exeter many smoothered in the snow. From almost every part of the western road, we have the like dreadful news, which all happened upon the very same day, and the truth thereof ready to be testified by hundreds that are since returned to this city, besides the carriers herein mentioned, who are themselves men of great credit.

London: printed by George Larkin, at the Lower-End of Broad Street, next to London-Wall. 1685

The Floods of January 1915

EDITH OLIVIER

*In 1912 Miss Olivier left Wilton Rectory and went with
her father to live in a house in Salisbury Close which was
earmarked for the senior prebendary. There she remained
for seven years until Canon Olivier died. This description
from her autobiography,* Without Knowing Mr
Walkley, *recalls a memorable start to the year 1915.*

It was the month of January 1915, and the unceasing rain of
that first autumn of the war had turned the five chalk streams
which meet at Salisbury into five raging torrents which no
hatches could control. At the same time, an exceptionally high
spring-tide rushed up the Avon from the sea. The water could
not get away. It broadened out upon the city.

The interior of the cathedral was even more lovely than the
Close outside. All through the night the water had been
silently coming up through the floor, and by morning the nave
was a large still pool, from which the pillars rose and into
which they threw their reflections. The medieval glass in the
west window made a tangled pattern of light and colour in the
water. The nave was quickly emptied of chairs and nothing
broke the beauty of its proportions.

The water did not reach the choir, and services were held

The interior of Salisbury Cathedral during the floods of
January 1915

there throughout the flood, the congregations reaching them upon perilous bridges made of planks. There were none of these on that first morning when my father and Dr Bourne, another very old canon, arrived for the service, having somehow made their way across the Close. These intrepid veterans were not deterred by the sight of that lake of cold-looking water. They were bent for the vestry which lay beyond it and they meant to get there. Each mounted a chair and armed himself with a second, which he planted in the water in front of him. On to this he now stepped, and then swung into position in front of it the chair he had just vacated. By repeating this manoeuvre the two fearless canons made stepping-stones for themselves from west to east of the cathedral.

The second day of the flood was the Festival of the Epiphany. At eight o'clock that morning, the Communion was celebrated in the Lady Chapel behind the choir. It was like the scene of a legendary shipwreck. The cathedral was almost in darkness, though here and there a gas jet threw a light which quivered in the water. As we crossed the plank bridges the faint reflections of the pillars swayed a little beneath us. The cathedral looked much larger than usual – empty, dark, and filled with water; and as Bishop Ridgeway came to the altar, the candlelight fell upon him in his shining cope and mitre, with the Pastoral Staff carried before him. He looked like some little elfin being.

During this flood of 1915, several of the Salisbury streets were flooded and people went about them by boat. Gina Fisher and I decided that it would be a historic feat to be rowed down Fisherton Street, so we set off for the starting-point, each accompanied by a scoffing sister to watch. I blush to say that our hearts failed us at the crucial moment. We found that there was a considerable gap between the last dry spot where it was possible to walk, and the point where the water was deep

A small boat conveys passengers along Fisherton Street, Salisbury, during the 1915 floods witnessed by Edith Olivier

enough to float a boat. Stout policemen carried the would-be passengers across this no-man's land – a most ridiculous sight, which all day attracted a large and hilarious crowd. But this was not the worst. The boat itself was so wet and dirty that no-one dared to sit down in it. Everyone had to stand, each man clutching at his nearest neighbour when the boat lurched suddenly. An unexpectedly big lurch always sent two or three people into the water, so that the lookers-on had plenty of fun for their money. We watched the scene for some time and then we agreed that although we had been right to think that this would be a historic occasion, yet it was better to watch history in the making than to make it ourselves.

The Great
Wiltshire Storm of
1859

A.C. SMITH

Revd Alfred Smith, vicar of Yatesbury near Calne, was a respected ornithologist and archaeologist, and for forty years he edited the Wiltshire Archaeological Magazine. *This article, which I have abridged, appeared in the issue for April 1860 and gives an eye-witness account of a tornado which had ploughed across north Wiltshire on the penultimate afternoon of 1859.*

The close of the year 1859 will long be remembered by the inhabitants of some of the villages of North Wilts. as the period of 'the Great Storm'. It occurred at about half-past one p.m. on Friday, December 30th, and beginning its devastations about a mile to the south of Calne, and coming up for [from?] the west, it shaped its course for E.N.E., and took nearly a straight line in that direction for about thirteen miles, its breadth varying from 250 to about 400 yards: at what velocity it rushed over this course it is impossible to conjecture, but it seems to be universally allowed that from two to three minutes was the time occupied in passing over any given spot; and during these few moments, it swept a clear and most perceptible path in its onward progress, tearing up by the roots and snapping short off the huge trunks of some of the largest elms and other trees, unroofing houses, stacks, and cottages, and hurling men and cattle to the ground, and dashing them furiously to and fro, and rolling them over and over in its rough embrace.

The first intimation we have of its assuming any great force is on the property of the Marquis of Lansdowne, near the Devizes road, about a mile south of Calne, where it broke off the large branch of an oak tree within the precincts of Bowood Park; thence, steering eastwards, it partially tore off the thatch of a cottage; blew down three trees at Stock Street, the property of Mr Robert Henley; and passed on to the Rookery Farm, where it also prostrated several fine elms and decapitated others. Thence to Quemerford Villa, astonishing the inmates by bursting in the door and windows: and so on to Mr Slade's Mill. Here it scattered far and wide the stone tiles of the roofing of the stables and other buildings, in addition to other damage. And now hurling down several trees on its way, it reached Blacklands Park, hitherto renowned for its magnificent timber. First it partially unroofed the new lodge, and snapped off many of the firs which formed a shelter at its back, then rushing forth into the Park, swept down no less than 148 trees, some of great size and beauty, tearing up some by the roots, and snapping off other large trunks, as if they had been twigs; so that to the inmates of the house, who were looking from the windows, and who were slightly removed from the main line of the storm, it appeared as if all the trees in the Park were simultaneously, and in an instant dashed headlong to the earth.

But the work of desolation goes on apace now, and away goes the storm, leaving Blacklands far behind, along the Bath road. Here it seems to have rushed up the gully, along which the greater part of the village of Cherhill is built. A few of the most prominent particulars in this locality may exemplify its violence: and first Cherhill Mill deserves especial mention, no less than fifty trees having been thrown down within a very small space; and yet Mr Reynolds the miller (who in passing to the mill could not reach it before the storm was upon him, and clung to a rail of the orchard during its entire passage) assures me that he neither heard nor saw a single tree fall, so awful and bewildering was the effect of its sudden tremendous and deafening attack. Again, in another instance, the roof of a cottage was lifted off in a mass and deposited in the road.

And now 'Excelsior' was the battle cry of the hurricane, and with a shriek of victory and a roar of exultation it rushed up the narrow ravine at the extreme east end of Cherhill, and on and away for the open down; and chancing to fall in with a wheat rick which stood in its path, it carried the greater part along with it, hurling whole sheaves several hundred yards, threshing out the corn all over the field, and whirling large quantities of straw above a mile. Spying six large trees standing out on the exposed plain, it hurled five of them to the ground like ninepins, and then on it dashed towards Yatesbury, which was to be the principal scene of its triumph. And first, singling out here and there a fir tree in some long plantations and belts on my glebe, it snapped them off or tore them up, to the number of forty, with most fantastic partiality, as if sending out a whiff for the purpose, as the main body of the storm hurried by, and leaving the surrounding trees apparently unruffled by the breeze. Thence, abstaining from the slightest injury to the Church, and scarcely removing a tile from the School, it began a furious onslaught on the timber all around, uprooting one of the large yews on my glebe, but sparing the pride of our churchyard, (which without partiality I believe to be the finest and best grown yew tree in the county) and overturning right and left, on either

The great yew tree in Yatesbury churchyard, near Calne,
which survived the storm of 1859, and is still flourishing

side of the church, the large trees which were the ornament of that portion of the parish.

Then straight away for Mr John Tanner's and the south end of the village, where it did more damage than in any other spot on its whole course: for first it entirely unroofed several cottages, ricks and barns: then threw down chimneys and outhouses: lifted off in a mass the entire roof of a long cattle-shed: smashed in the windows on the south front of the house: laid flat the east and west walls of the kitchen garden: prostrated two barns: and uprooted or broke off almost all the fine elms round the house: in addition to the playful freaks of throwing a cow into a pond, hurling one of the large cart horses from one end of the yard to the other, and dashing him at length against the shed at the extreme end; and as a climax, taking up a heavy broad-wheeled waggon weighing 22 cwt., and lifting it over a high hedge, depositing it on its side a dozen yards or more from where it stood. After these eccentric manoeuvres and wondrous feats of strength, away goes the hurricane for Winterbourne Monkton, coursing again for two miles over open country, and only marking its path here and there by overthrowing the few trees which stood in its way.

Most mercifully not a single life was lost, nor did any serious accident occur to either man or beast. Hair-breadth escapes indeed there were in abundance: for instance, several men and boys were buried under the ruins of fallen barns both at Yatesbury and Monkton, and how they all escaped the heavy beams and rafters which fell all around them, seems perfectly miraculous, but they were all extricated from their perilous position with no worse result than sundry bruises and an exceeding terror. Still more remarkable are some of the instances of narrow escape of destruction among the cattle. At the extreme west of Cherhill, near Mr Maundrell's farm, lies a narrow strip of meadow of about half an acre in extent, surrounded with elms, no less than 23 of which were swept down in an instant, and appeared completely to choke up the field; yet it will hardly be believed that a donkey belonging to the carpenter, Charles Aland, who dwells hard by, and which had been turned into this meadow, was found unhurt amidst the prostrate timber, though there appeared scarcely a vacant space wherein it could stand. Nor was this the only animal bearing a charmed life which the worthy carpenter possessed, for a large tree fell across his pig-sty, crushing it to the earth, but the pig crept out uninjured, and was found standing by its ruined home perfectly untouched. I have already remarked on the overthrow of Mr Tanner's cart horse and cow at Yatesbury; but when the storm was gone by, they seem to have emerged, the one from the shed into which he was whirled, the other out of the pond into which she was cast, none the worse for their temporary discomfiture. Indeed the only creatures which seem to have lost their lives in the hurricane, were sundry hares and partridges, three or four of the former having been picked up dead, immediately after the storm, and I myself having chanced to ride by some of the latter, which I found almost entirely denuded of feathers, doubtless the effect of their being repeatedly dashed with violence on the earth.

I come now to speak of the hail-stones which accompanied the storm in large quantities, and which from their enormous size and peculiar shapes were almost as extraordinary as the tornado itself: moreover, their forms seem to have varied in different localities; thus Mr Spenser of Bowood saw some more resembling flat pieces of ice than hail: they were nearly half an inch in thickness, and from two to three inches in diameter, star-shaped, with rays ranging from four to seven in number, and the rays of different sizes. Others again were wedge-shaped and about three inches in length, and in some cases several of these were frozen together. At Yatesbury the hailstones were of an entirely different shape, for they had now lost their wedge-like character, and resembled rough irregular stones of about two inches in diameter, and this form may perhaps have been produced by their being whirled about and retarded in their fall, when the storm was at its greatest violence. At Cherhill there was little or no hail, but to the north on the hill above they fell freely, and I have a graphic description of their shape from Mr Neate's shepherd, who likened them to the middle of a waggon wheel, with the spokes all broken off. At Monkton no hail was seen, though there was an abundance of rain, but at Berwick Bassett the hailstones fell in large quantities, and for their enormous size I am happy to be able to adduce the testimony of the Rev R. Mead and Mr Viveash, who measured some and found them to be $4\frac{3}{4}$ inches, and others again, measured accurately with compasses, proved to be no less than $5\frac{1}{2}$ inches, and some even to have exceeded 6 inches in circumference, with a diameter of half an inch.

I regret that I have no means of ascertaining the precise amount of rain which fell during the hurricane, but that a very copious discharge then took place is certain, and by way of obtaining the nearest information on this head within my reach, I have instituted enquiries at all the mills near which it passed, and from one and all I derive the same reply, that the rise of the water was both greater and more sudden than was ever remembered on any former occasion of other heavy rains: this is the unanimous opinion of the millers at Cherhill, Quemerford, and Blacklands Mills, where, though within a mile of the source of the stream which turned them, it was found necessary to draw the hatches and stop the works for a time, on account of the rush of water which bore down with irresistible fury immediately after the storm had passed by.

I should add that the day of our hurricane was marked throughout by sudden and violent gusts of wind, accompanied with hail and rain in heavy showers; those who were hunting with the Duke of Beaufort at Bremhill on that day will not readily forget the hail-stones, which descended with such force

as to cut their hands till their knuckles bled, and to make their horses kick and plunge from the pain inflicted by them. Still more will the day be remembered in England as the disastrous day of storm, which cost her the life of one of her best officers, the gallant Captain Harrison of the Great Eastern. While those of the inhabitants of North Wilts. who live within its limits, will never forget to the last day of their lives 'the great Wiltshire storm of December 30th, 1859'.

The Passing of the Year

ALFRED WILLIAMS

That's Christmas over, then, and the old year is drawing to a close. We shall turn again to Alfred Williams, but not this time as folklorist or reporter. Here are two sonnets by Alfred Williams the poet, written on New Year's Eve 1910.

The air hangs dull and heavy; not a breath
   Stirs in the poplar pointing bare and high,
   No scarce-heard sound or whisper, not a sigh
Escapes, and silent is the world beneath;
Calm flows the river; in many a twining wreath

Salisbury. The Close Gate. Inner View.

*With best wishes for a happy
New Year from*

31.12.1902

Winnie.

This postcard was franked at Salisbury, 10.15 p.m. on New
Year's Eve 1902, on its way to an address in Brighton

· A Wiltshire Christmas ·

Down from the elmtree pillar standing by
   The verdant ivy droops; leaden the sky;
All nature's buried in the gloom of death.
'Tis the year's parting sorrow, for he grieves
   And suffers inner anguish, like to one
   Viewing Time's happiness for ever gone.
But lo! as the old dweller darkly leaves,
A new inheritor the rule receives,
   And other joys come rushing endless on.

'Tis but a step to midnight; one stroke more,
   One fleeting space for sorrows and farewells,
   One last look backward where high Memory dwells,
Then in the untrodden path that lies before
We must push onward, ever to that shore
   Toward which our utmost fate draws and compels.
   Hark! from the starlit tower the merry bells
Peal as they've pealed a thousand times of yore.
All this is banished, whether good or ill;
   Our joys and sufferings, our toils and pains
   Diminish, our life's star waxes and wanes.
Ere the dark wave close o'er us, deep and still,
Let us go forth, fearless in mind and will,
   And grapple with the future that remains.

The Myth of the Old-Fashioned Christmas?

But what was it really like at Christmas one hundred years ago? Not so very different, perhaps. There were the school parties, the traffic, the pantomimes, the present-buying, the latest posting times, drinks with the neighbours, happy times, unhappy times, even tragic times. Here to round off our dip into the world of Wiltshire Christmas past is a selection of reports, all drawn from local newspapers of the period 1890–2.

CHRISTMAS AND THE POST OFFICE: As Christmas Day this year falls on a Sunday, the attention of the public is urgently called to the necessity of posting there [*sic*] letters, Christmas cards, and parcels early, in order that Sunday work may be reduced within the smallest possible limits, and delivery in due time ensured. To attain these results letters, cards, and parcels should be posted by the 22nd, or at all events not later than the 23rd December.

TREAT TO SCHOOL CHILDREN: The Mayor (Mr G.H. Mead) on Friday evening entertained the children attending the [Devizes] British Schools to a tea, in the Corn Exchange.

· A Wiltshire Christmas ·

The Mayor and Mayoress of Salisbury, Councillor and Mrs S.
Chalk, switch on the Odeon's Christmas tree lights in 1951,
while the cinema's children's choir sing carols

There were three long rows of tables extending the whole
length of the hall and each was crowded. There were over 500
children present. The tea was supplied by Mr Stevens and Mr
Ellen, and a number of ladies and gentlemen, including the
Mayor and the Mayoress and the teachers waited. For more
than an hour the children, with children's appetites, kept their
attendants exceedingly busy. Plenty of bread and butter and
cake was supplied, and was put away with astonishing celerity
to the accompaniment of a band in the gallery and a babel of
voices below. After a long time the unrestrained prompting to
satisfy the demands of autocratic stomachs became less active
and on the other hand vociferation became more loud and
insuppressible. In due time all were satisfied, and then the

tables were removed and games of various kinds were indulged in and were superintended by the Mayor, Mayoress, teachers, and other friends of the school. After an evening's fun, which will be remembered for a long time, the children separated, not without cheers loud and prolonged for the Mayor and Mayoress, who had so thoughtfully remembered the little ones and contributed to their happiness in the season of good-will.

CHRISTMAS AT CALNE WORKHOUSE: Great pains were taken to brighten the lot of the 84 inmates on Christmas day. In the morning each inmate was presented with a Christmas card and letter, generously provided by Miss Wickham, of Bournemouth. The dining-hall and wards were very prettily decorated for the occasion. The dinner consisted of roast beef and plum pudding, of which there was a liberal supply; one pint of ale was served to each adult, and in addition one ounce of tobacco was distributed to each man, and half an ounce of snuff to the women, the children and those in the sick wards receiving oranges and sweets. Mr T. Harris sent a present of one shilling each to the men, ninepence to the women, and sixpence to the children. Mr and Mrs E.R. Henly, Mr and Mrs T. Harris, together with several ladies and gentlemen of the neighbourhood, were present in the dining-hall. In addition to the above Lord Henry Bruce, MP, sent a liberal supply of tobacco for the men; a quarter of a pound of tea, one pound of lump sugar, and half an ounce of snuff for each woman; and plum cake, oranges and sweets for the children. After tea, the master, matron, porter and nurse, together with the inmates, assembled in the dining-hall, where the children sang several Christmas carols, and a number of well-rendered songs and recitations were given, a very pleasant and enjoyable evening being brought to a close by the singing of the National Anthem. Cheers were given in very hearty fashion for the guardians, Lord Henry Bruce, Mr T. Harris, and the master and matron, after which the inmates retired to their respective rooms, apparently happy and contented, and grateful for the kindness that had been bestowed upon them.

Christmas 1911 being celebrated at the Salisbury Union Workhouse, which stood in Coombe Road, Harnham, on the outskirts of Salisbury

ELEGANT AND USEFUL HOLIDAY GIFTS: The gift a person makes is in keeping with the taste and thought of the individual who makes it. Expense has nothing to do with it. In this age many pretty and useful things are not expensive. A common person may make a common present, but one with a refined mind will always exercise good taste and good sense in what he gives. It is a mistake to throw away money on gifts which are useless, for while they may give pleasure to the recipient, the only gifts which afford anything more than a passing pleasure are those which are useful. Among the latter class are good instructive books, or better still, some useful toilet requisite, like a box of Toilet 'Vinolia' Soap, which cannot fail to please, and is strongly recommended for winter use by medical men to keep the skin smooth and free from roughness. The Vestal Vinolia Soap is also a charming article.

A BEDDING MANUFACTURER SHOT BY A MAN OF INDEPEN-DENT MEANS AT BROUGHTON GIFFORD.

Unfortunately the story is far less interesting than the headline!

DRAMATIC PERFORMANCES AT FISHERTON HOUSE ASYLUM: On Wednesday evening a very successful dramatic enter-tainment was given in the Theatre Royal, Fisherton House, by the officers and nurses connected with the asylum. The hall was quite full, a large number of visitors attending, through the kindness of Dr Finch. The evening's programme took the form of the 'triple bill', which some London theatres found so popular last season, and consisted of three farces, namely, *My Wife's Second Floor*, *Popping the Question*, and *Nursey Chickweed*. All three went with great vigour, but the last especially kept the audience in roars of laughter. Such a high level of excellence was reached all round that it is impossible to single out any individual performance, but it can safely be said that the members of the 'corps dramatique' at Fisherton House surpassed themselves and eclipsed all previous records. Amongst the ladies, Miss E. Browning was very successful in the parts of Miss Topheavy and Miss Winterblossom, and is to be specially commended for the clear enunciation of her lines. Miss S. Chalke found a congenial part as Bobbin, the housemaid in *Popping the Question*, and both sang and acted with great vivacity. Miss Chalke is to be complimented on the effective quaintness of her costume in this piece, fitting the character exactly. Miss Ford played the part of Miss Biffen, the old maid desirous of matrimony, in the same piece exceedingly well, and her dress was one of the most effective ever seen on these boards. In fact all the designers of the costumes in this farce deserve great praise for the taste and suitability of their creations. One of the hits of the evening was made by Miss Bruce Dibben as the hoyden Nelly Mountsorrel in *Nursey Chickweed*. Miss Dibben evidently entered fully into the spirit of the thing, and gave a most lively rendering of the part, her final transformation into a boy being a great success. Of the male characters Dr Slater made a spirited Captain Topheavy, and got as much out of the part as was possible. Mr Newman, as Barnes, the miller, was a very good rustic, and as the duplicate Nursey Chickweed, so changed the fashion of his face that his own friends did not know him. Mr Fanner was, as usual, the life and soul of the scenes in which he appeared, but was evidently most appreciated as Nursey Chickweed, whose absurdly farcical prevarications cause so much amusement. During the intervals Miss S. Chalke sang 'All in a Garden Fair', and 'The Carnival', in a very charming and sympathetic manner, and Mr Fanner gave excellent renderings of 'The 7th Royal Fusiliers' (in which the participation of his two little girls added greatly to the effect), and as an encore 'I couldn't'. The accompaniments were played by Mrs Chapman, Mr Trowbridge led the incidental music by the band, and everything on the stage went smoothly under the efficient management of Dr R.T. Finch.

WILTON GOSSIP: For some portion of the Xmas holidays 'Nemo' [the Wilton correspondent's pseudonym] has been buried in deep thought. Seated in the chair of reflection, with knitted brow and thoughtful aspect, I remained insensible to the sounds of festive mirth and clinking glasses; even the

pleasurable anticipation of certain osculatory performances, which had previously filled me with the wildest excitement, faded from my imagination as completely as if labial juxta-position was the most formal and uninteresting of duties. The cause of this all absorbing forgetfulness was the following questions, which, when placed in my hand, I was directed to get answered with verbatim truth, and as I have struggled with them alone in the solitude of my own sanctum and miserably failed, I place them before my gossip friends whose intelligent and comprehensive perceptions may bring a different result. They are as follows:

1. Is it true that the Technical Education Committee and the Ratepayers' Association are hibernating together?
2. If not, are they both alive and well, and what is their present address?
3. Has the Town Band got any enemies?
4. Is it right to conclude that because some of our corporate authority seem to appear ignorant of certain complaints that they are necessarily of the order pachydermata?
5. Is it true that the Guardians are putting a fence round their pig sty to keep out the swine fever?
6. How is it that the gas and other connections of the underground system of piping of the town get lost directly they are wanted?
7. Would it be advisable to put a stick in to mark the place, when found, for future convenience?. . .
12. If all the true Liberals of Wilton have become blue, what shade has [*sic*] the original blues taken?. . .
16. What is to be done with the present paving stones of North Street during the proposed alterations?

· *A Wiltshire Christmas* ·

All correct and authoritative answers to the above will be published at the usual rates – see scale of charges. Postal Orders preferred.

St John's Square, Wilton, during the floods of December 1910

CHRISTMAS TRAFFIC ON THE GREAT WESTERN RAILWAY: On the Great Western Railway there was scarcely a train throughout Christmas week which was not laden to its utmost capacity, even when duplicated, as most of the long-journey trains were after the Saturday previous. On Christmas Eve 8,600 passengers were booked at Paddington Station alone this year, against 7,810 last year. Cheap tickets were issued to Bath, Bristol, Taunton, Ilfracombe, Exeter, Torquay, Plymouth, Falmouth, Penzance, Yeovil, Dorchester, Weymouth, and other stations in the West of England and Weymouth districts, and no fewer than 2,600 persons availed themselves of the facilities thus afforded. On Christmas Eve a special train left Paddington at 10 pm for New Milford [now Neyland, opposite Pembroke Dock] and called at the principal stations en route, while another for Reading, Swindon, Bath, Bristol, and the West of England left at 11.50 pm. The 9 pm mail train from Paddington to Penzance ran in two parts on Monday, Tuesday, and Wednesday; passengers and the company's parcels only were conveyed by the first part, the second part being devoted entirely to the mails and parcel post traffic. In addition to the parcel post, which every year becomes heavier and more difficult to handle, the company's own parcel traffic was very exacting, and special trains were run for its accommodation between London and Plymouth, Birkenhead and New Milford, and the principal intermediate stations. For the convenience of passengers returning after the holidays special trains were run to London on Monday last.

MR ARCHER'S PANTOMIME: Messrs Roberts, Archer, and Bartlett's Company, who are invariably well received in Salisbury, appeared in their annual Christmas pantomime at the County Hall on Thursday evening, to commence a three nights' engagement, in addition to a matinée today (Saturday). At the opening performance there was a crowded house, every seat, with the exception of a few at the front, being occupied. Over 1000 persons must therefore have been present. The subject of the pantomime was *Aladdin and the Wonderful Lamp*, which lent itself to extremely picturesque treatment, of which the author, Mr C.J. Archer, took full advantage, some of the scenes, the whole of which were new, being gorgeous displays of the features of Chinese life, while the jewelled cave was a masterpiece of brilliant perspective. The transformation scene, representing 'The Seasons' was also very pretty and bright, though lacking somewhat in elaboration. Of the pantomime itself it is impossible, with one or two exceptions, to speak too

· A Wiltshire Christmas ·

·⊹· MRS. JARLEY'S WAX WORKS. ·⊹·

AN EXHIBITION

OF THE ABOVE WORLD-FAMED

WAX WORKS

Will be given at the

SAMBOURNE SCHOOLROOMS,

WARMINSTER,

On the Evenings of Thursday and Friday, Dec. 21st & 22nd.

This Collection numbers amongst its Curiosities

The Chinese Giant.

The Bearded Woman

Mrs. Winslow's Soothing Syrup.

Robinson Crusoe.

The Babes in the Wood.

Joan of Arc.

THE USUAL ORCHESTRA WILL ACCOMPANY THE EXHIBITION.

Mrs. JARLEY has kindly consented to allow the proceeds of her Unrivalled Entertainment to be devoted to MUTUAL Improvement and SCHOOLROOM Improvement.

Price of Admission—on Thursday Evening, 2s. and 1s.; on Friday Evening, 1s. and 6d.

Doors open at 7.30. Exhibition opens at 8.

Carriages ordered at 10 precisely.

B. W. Coates, "Journal" Office, Warminster.

A leaflet advertising Mrs Jarley's wax works, a Christmas treat for Warminster, probably in 1883

153

highly. The cast was strong, and the costumes, which add so much to the effect of such performances, were exceedingly rich and appropriate. Mr C.J. Archer, although acting under the pseudonym of 'Miss Emily Jones', was easily recognised in the character of 'Widow Mustapha', which he assumed with much droll humour. Mr J. Malcolm Dunn was, as in former years, a host in himself, and Mr H.G. Williams, Mr Sydney Oldham, and Mr H. Lucca filled their respective parts creditably. Miss Ettie Levanne was a vivacious Aladdin, and the various Genii of the Lamp and Ring were ably led by the Continental dancers, the Sisters Bateman. The play included a clever musical sketch by Mr Arthur Learto, who was also the clown in the finale, when some lively and novel stage business was introduced. One or two of the songs were objectionable, and might with propriety be divested of some of their verses. At the close of the entertainment there was a loud outburst of applause. The interest of the audience had been well sustained throughout, though there was a general feeling that the ballets had not been quite so varied and numerous as usual.

WILCOT, PLEASANT GATHERINGS: On New Year's Day, Mrs Davidson, of West Stowell, gave the children of the day and Sunday schools, with their teachers and the members of the Girls' Friendly Society, a substantial tea of cake and buns, in the village schoolroom. After tea, a fine Christmas tree was unveiled, laden with pretty toys, work-boxes, knives, and other useful things. Each child was presented with a present from the tree by Colonel and Mrs Davidson. At the close of the proceedings, the children gave ringing cheers for those who had provided them with such a treat, and also for the Misses Smelt and other friends who had waited on them. The National Anthem was then sung, and as the children left the room each received two oranges, a basket of sweets and some crackers.

A Swindon tramcar outside the Town Hall, Regent Circus,
during blizzard conditions in 1908

The next day, January 2nd, being Major Trafford's
birthday, that gallant officer gave his usual treat to all the
villagers above 16 years of age *{presumably the children stayed at
home to play with their knives}*. At 6 o'clock they assembled at
Stowell Park House, where a sumptuous meat tea was
provided for them. All present were well entertained by Mrs
Trafford, Miss Austin, the Major, Captain Greenwood, Mr
Greenwood, and Mr Austin. After partaking of the good
things, the Major's health was drunk with hearty cheers, all
present wishing him many happy returns of the day. He
suitably responded, saying it gave him much pleasure to
welcome them once more. He was sorry to say there were
several old faces missing, but some new ones appeared.
Wishing them a happy and prosperous new year, he expressed
a hope that they would enjoy themselves. The rest of the
evening was spent in songs, recitations, and dancing; 'God
save the Queen' being sung at the close of the proceedings,
which were most enjoyable throughout.

Acknowledgements

It is my great pleasure to acknowledge the friendly and untiring help of the staffs of the Wiltshire County Council, Library & Museum Service Headquarters Local Studies Library and Salisbury Local Studies Library; the Wiltshire Record Office; and the Wiltshire Archaeological & Natural History Society Library. Special thanks to Felicity Gilmour and Katie Jordan for their help with folklore, to Andrew Crookston for his help with George Atwood's handwriting, and to Alison for never-failing encouragement and support.

'Christmas comes to a Wiltshire Village' is from *Wiltshire Village* (1939) by Heather and Robin Tanner, by permission of Heather Tanner and Impact Books. 'Dull Dark Days' and 'The Floods of January 1915' are from *Without knowing Mr Walkley* (1939) by Edith Olivier, by permission of her neice, Miss Rosemary Olivier. 'Soft Weather' is from *Flowers in the Grass* (1920) by Maurice Hewlett. 'Mog' is from *Further up the Crossing* (1987) by Ken Ausden, by permission of the author and Redbrick Publishing. 'Christmas Pudding and other Hazards' is by John Chandler, drawing on material in *Wiltshire Folklore* (1975) by Kathleen Wiltshire, *The Folklore of Wiltshire* (1976) by Ralph Whitlock, and articles in *W{iltshire} A{rchaeological and Natural History} M{agazine}* vols. 14, p. 328, 50, pp. 27-37, and *Wiltshire Notes and Queries* vol. 1, p. 151. 'The Mummers' is from *Swindon: Reminiscences . . .* (1885) by William Morris. 'Stourton Customs' is from 'In a Wiltshire Village' by E.E. Balch, in *The Antiquary* vol. 44, pp. 379-82. 'The Cricklade Wassail' is from 'Old Time Customs of North Wiltshire' by Alfred Williams, in *North Wilts. Herald*, 21.12.1928. 'The Boy Bishop of Salisbury' is by John Chandler, drawing on *The Boy Bishop at Salisbury and elsewhere* (1921) by J.M.J. Fletcher, and *Sarum Close* (1938) by Dora H. Robertson. 'A Party to Remember' is from *The Wandering Years: Diaries 1922-1939* (1961) by Cecil Beaton, by permission of the Literary Executors of Sir Cecil Beaton, and Rupert Crew Ltd. 'Evaporated Apricots and Plain Grosvenor' is taken from a catalogue in the Dewey Museum, Warminster (D620), through the kindness of Jack Field and Danny Howell, and by permission of the Warminster History Society. 'Tha Girt Big Figgetty Pooden' and 'Tha Snow' are from *The Wiltshire Moonrakers edition of West Countrie Rhymes* (1903) by Edward Slow. 'The Grand-Master's Dinner' and 'Christmas Carol for the Year 1780' by Michael Burrough are in the Wiltshire Record Office (WRO 473/381), and are published by permission of the County Archivist, Steven Hobbs. 'One Person, Drinking' is from *Life in an English Village* (1909) by Maud F. Davies. 'The Awdrys' Jolly Party' is from *Kilvert's Diary*, vol. 2 (1939), edited by William Plomer. 'Carol Singing at Berwick St James' is from *Moonrakings* (1930), edited by Edith Olivier and M.K.S. Edwards. 'Wiltshire Carols' is derived from 'The Folk Carol in Wiltshire' by Alfred Williams, in *Wiltshire Gazette*, 29.12.1927; *Wiltshire Folk Songs and Carols* (1890) by Geoffrey Hill; and *WAM* vol. 50, pp. 36-7. 'Christmas' is from *The Temple* (1634) by George Herbert. 'The Other Wise Man' is from *Marlborough and Other Poems* (1916) by Charles Hamilton Sorley. 'Old Elijah' is from *Round about the Upper Thames* (1922) by Alfred Williams. 'Christmas Eve at Sutton Evias' is from *The Gentleman of the Party* (1936) by A.G. Street, by permission of his daughter, Pamela Street. 'The Christmas Day Sequence' is from *The Sarum Missal in English* (1868). 'An Outing for Angels' is from *Gallipot Eyes: a Wiltshire Diary* (1976) by Elspeth Huxley, by permission of the author. 'Christmas without Daddy' is from *By Safe Hand: the Letters of Sybil and David Eccles* (1983), by permission of the authors and The Bodley Head. 'The Evacuees' Party' by Ena Berrett is in the Wiltshire Record Office (WRO 1442/1), and is published by permission of the author, and the County Archivist, Steven Hobbs. 'A Day of Black Disaster' by George Atwood is in the Wiltshire Record Office (WRO 1229/1), and is published by permission of the County Archivist, Steven Hobbs. 'Christmas Ale and a Sad Nativity' is by John Chandler, quoting extracts and translations from documents in the Wiltshire Record Office (WRO 651/1, WRO 522/1). 'Gastard Sunday Morning' is by John Chandler. 'Footprints at Longleat' is from *The Year Returns* (1952) by Elizabeth Hamilton, by permission of the author. 'Skating' is from *The Hills and the Vale* (1909) by Richard Jefferies. 'A True Relation' was reprinted in *The Late Flood . . . an account of the Disastrous Inundation . . .* (1841) (photocopy in Local Studies Library, Trowbridge). 'The Great Wiltshire Storm of 1859' by A.C. Smith is abridged from *WAM* vol. 6, pp.365-89. 'The Passing of the Year' is from *Poems in Wiltshire* (1911) by Alfred Williams. 'The Myth of the Old-Fashioned Christmas?' was compiled by John Chandler from the following newspapers: *Salisbury Journal*, 17.12.1892; *Devizes and Wiltshire Gazette*, 22.12.1892; *Marlborough Times*, 3.1.1891; *Salisbury Journal*, 24.12.1892; *Devizes and Wiltshire Gazette*, 22.12.1892; *Salisbury Journal*, 24.12.1892; *Salisbury Times*, 8.1.1892; *Marlborough Times*, 3.1.1891; *Salisbury Journal* 9.1.1892; *Marlborough Times*, 10.1.1891.

Picture Credits

I am most grateful to Derek Parker for his expert processing of my own photographs (JHC); to Brian Bridgeman and the Swindon Society (BB/SS), David Buxton (DB), and Peter Daniels (PRD) for supplying me with photographs; and to Ena Berrett and Jack Field (RJF) for allowing me to copy photographs.

Page 4 DB; 10 JHC; 12 BB/SS / Mr Denis Bird; 22 BB/SS / Mr Denis Bird; 27 DB; 37 JHC; 43 BB/SS / Mrs B. MacDonald; 49 PRD / Mr Albert Noyce; 52 PRD; 62 JHC; 66 PRD / *Salisbury Journal*; 72 JHC; 75 JHC; 87 JHC / RJF and Warminster History Society; 98 JHC; 102 JHC / Miss Ena Berrett; 105 JHC / RJF and Warminster History Society; 107 PRD; 108 JHC; 113 BB/SS / Mr Denis Bird; 116 JHC; 119 JHC; 124 DB; 128 BB/SS/ Mr Tony Daglish; 131 PRD; 133 PRD; 137 JHC; 142 JHC; 145 PRD / *Salisbury Journal*; 147 PRD; 151 PRD; 153 JHC / RJF and Warminster History Society; 155 BB/SS / Mr Denis Bird.